I0414775

A Square of Daffodils, Capitalism, and Why Children Don't Learn

A Square of Daffodils, Capitalism, and
Why Children Don't Learn
The Story of Building a Wonderful, Loving Family

Harold L. Doerr

iUniverse, Inc.
Bloomington

A Square of Daffodils, Capitalism, and Why Children Don't Learn
The Story of Building a Wonderful, Loving Family

Copyright © 2011 by Harold L. Doerr

All rights reserved. No part of this book may be used or reproduced by any means, graphic, electronic, or mechanical, including photocopying, recording, taping or by any information storage retrieval system without the written permission of the publisher except in the case of brief quotations embodied in critical articles and reviews.

iUniverse books may be ordered through booksellers or by contacting:

iUniverse
1663 Liberty Drive
Bloomington, IN 47403
www.iuniverse.com
1-800-Authors (1-800-288-4677)

Because of the dynamic nature of the Internet, any web addresses or links contained in this book may have changed since publication and may no longer be valid. The views expressed in this work are solely those of the author and do not necessarily reflect the views of the publisher, and the publisher hereby disclaims any responsibility for them.

Any people depicted in stock imagery provided by Thinkstock are models, and such images are being used for illustrative purposes only.

Certain stock imagery © Thinkstock.

ISBN: 978-1-4502-9340-2 (sc)
ISBN: 978-1-4502-9342-6 (hc)
ISBN: 978-1-4502-9341-9 (e)

Printed in the United States of America

iUniverse rev. date: 07/15/2011

Dedicated to my son Jerald and his family, Ivonne and Darius.

Thanks to Suzanne Geba, colleague and friend
for her help and encouragement.

Introduction

While examining my life and considering my learning and teaching experiences, I concluded that family is very important in this process, so Part I of my writing is about my family and their move westward.

Part II details my life story, family experiences, dealing with a learning disability, and having quite a variety of teaching and learning experiences, as well as adopting a child.

Part III explores how I believe capitalism has negatively influenced learning in this country, and why it is almost impossible to evaluate teachers and schools. When we hear groups say that we want government out of our lives, they really mean that we don't want government to control what we pay our employees or how much we pollute, and never mind making us clean up or pay for the pollution we create.

There are many pundits and politicians who have never taught, or even spent time in what they refer to as failing schools, who criticize these schools and teachers. These people are not qualified to make these judgments and they do a great deal of damage.

Part I

My Family

Introduction

Each family group seems to have created special places for the extended family to gather. The buildings were not unusual, but what I remember most is never having any negative interactions or anyone ever arguing at any family gathering. I always felt as though they were gatherings of love and caring for each other.

The place where the family seemed to gather most often was on the Rogue River in Oregon, and my Dad's brother, Uncle Bob, created this place and he and Aunt Monica always made everyone welcome at any time. He started playing baseball with the Hollywood team in his mid-teens for two years, and then the team was moved to San Diego, where it became the San Diego Padres. He played in the first game the Padres ever played, and he became friends with the legendary Ted Williams. They both went on to the Boston Red Sox, and Uncle Bob is now the oldest living person in the baseball hall of fame.

While he was playing for the Padres, he bought property on the Rogue River in Oregon, and that is where he met and married Monica Terpin, a schoolteacher. They developed two different pieces of property there on the river, and they have been wonderful family gathering places for about three-quarters of a century.

Chapter 1
The River

Monica Terpin is on her knees planting daffodils around the little one-room schoolhouse at the edge of the clearing, with Foster Creek just to the south and the Rogue River curving a crescent around the east side of the clearing. The Big Bend Ranch, where she is boarding, is in view at the far north end, and the forest forms a dark green boundary on the west. Even though Monica is not yet twenty years old, she is a born teacher, and planning ahead, she knew that in the spring, these flowers, with their beautiful sun-filled, trumpet-shaped yellow centers, would welcome the end of winter.

The Big Bend Ranch

Illahe one room schoolhouse

This was 1935, also the year I was born. I realized in later years that one of the reasons I remembered so much about my life was because early in life I started reviewing each day's events as I was lying in bed before going to sleep each night.

Monica had taken the mail boat from Gold Beach, Oregon, up the Rogue River to Illahe, where she would teach in a one-room schoolhouse and begin a new and exciting journey in her life. Among her luggage on the boat that day was a small suitcase that had a hole in the side where a crank could be inserted so she could wind it up and play the large records. She knew that most of the children up in the wilderness had not heard music. Music would be a new and exciting experience for them, a new reason for some of them to come to school.

As the boat plied its way through the canyons and over the rough swells, the cold wind blew her red hair. She had to be fascinated by the sights of the forested mountains rising up on both sides of the river and the occasional flat-topped tree with the osprey nest built by those interesting birds that mate for life. There would have been many animals along the river's edge, having come out of the woods to drink, perhaps even a bear that came to catch one of the salmon that were so abundant, one of the things the river was famous for.

The farther the boat splashed up the river, the more desolate yet more beautiful it became. After a long trip, she would arrive at the place that would be home for a good part of her life.

It was common in those days for a room to be provided for the schoolteacher by one of the local residents and this was the case for Monica. She would be rooming with Mrs. Petinger at one end of a beautiful meadow, which she would walk across to get to her schoolhouse. Mrs. Petinger was a motherly type and would help dispel any loneliness she felt about being so far from home and in such an isolated, lonely place. The little, nearly square schoolhouse sat at the lower end of the meadow, with the river on one side and the forested mountain on the other side of the clearing. It was down near where Foster Creek splashed into the Rogue.

As soon as she got settled in her room, she wanted to see where she would be teaching, and she knew immediately that she wanted not only music inside the school but something inviting on the outside, so she ordered enough daffodil bulbs to go completely around the schoolhouse, and as soon as they came that fall, she planted them. She knew that when they bloomed in the spring, the bright gold color would not only add life to this place, but they would also tell her students something about her as a person, a beautiful person.

Daffodil bulbs multiply and come up each spring for many years to come, which hers have! The next spring, her students, knowing that she loved flowers, would bring bouquets of the beautiful wild yellow and blue iris and even a flower they called a lady's slipper, and sure enough, in later years, I found lady's slipper orchids growing along the banks of the river. I didn't know that orchids grew in colder climates, but apparently they do.

Aunt Monica with her students

About twelve of the sixteen students she would have were American Indians, and as Monica looked out the schoolhouse window, I am sure it was easy for her to imagine how the land must have looked when it was lived on and farmed, probably by the ancestors of the very children she would be teaching.

Over to the right, there would have been dugout canoes along the river, which had an abundance of fish, and in the forest to the left, there were many game animals—turkeys, deer, elk, and so forth. There were also freshwater springs. There would have been crops growing and teepees to live in. For many thousands of years, it would have been the perfect place to live.

We know Indians lived in the beautiful clearing for thousands of years, not because of the landfills, freeways, and things that will identify us to future people, but by the abundance of stones reshaped into the beautiful arrowheads that were found in abundance there. This land was no longer theirs to farm on, but they still lived nearby, and I am sure the older folks told stories of past life in such a beautiful place. Thousands of years of socialism that had worked so well had ended.

Chapter 2
The Ranch

Dad's paternal grandfather, John Doerr and his brother Phil came from Kansas, probably in the 1870s, and they both settled in the Santa Barbara-Carpinteria area of California. We don't know much else about his family, but he was a serious gambler and womanizer.

Dad's paternal grandmother, Emma Moncton, was born in Rutland, Vermont, and in the spring of 1876, at age twelve, she came with her family on the train to Sacramento, California. They then probably took a small boat to San Francisco, where they took a boat called the *Santa Maria* to Santa Barbara. The pier that they landed on is still used to this day. They went from there to Lompoc, where her father set up a machine shop run by a waterwheel.

John Doerr and Emma Moncton were married in the 1880s and had three children: Cora, Harold, and Violet. John was abusive to the children, and because of his gambling and womanizing problems, they finally separated.

When Harold, my grandfather, was about ten years old, his father kidnapped him and took him to work on the Baldwin Ranch at Santa Anita, east of Los Angeles, where he worked hard and slept in the barn.

His father took what money he earned and was quite abusive; he had been known to horsewhip him. His mother's brother found him and took him back to his mother.

When he was twelve years old, he was working at changing horses on the stage coach at Gaviota, above Santa Barbara, so that there would be fresh horses to pull the steep grade. He did not attend school for long, but he had a wealth of knowledge.

My great-grandmother Emma had a boardinghouse and a butcher shop, and when John lost them at the gambling table, she divorced him. There was a story that he once owned about half of what is now Santa Barbara and lost it all gambling. He remarried and had three more children, Tom, Stan, and Dorothy. In later years, Dorothy confided in family members that the reason she never married was that her father abused her so much.

James B. Smith, a tall, thin man, was a cooper (a barrel maker), and he made barrels to store the tar from the local tar pits in Carpinteria. He had been a boarder at Emma's rooming house, and he and Emma became friends. They married in 1900 and moved to Los Angeles. They bought ten acres of land east of Los Angeles, just west of San Dimas, and made plans for an orange grove. My grandfather was only thirteen years old, but he helped them clear the sagebrush and cactus off the land, and they planted potatoes the first year in order to afford to buy the orange trees. That year, my grandfather lived in a tent on the land to guard the potatoes from rabbits and other predators. The second year, the orange trees were planted.

In Southern California, crops must be irrigated much of the year, and my great-grandfather Smith had a hired handyman to supervise this chore. There must be a watchful eye to see when the irrigation water reaches the end of each ditch at the lower end of the grove, and then someone must go to the upper end of the grove, where the water standpipes are, to change the water into a new ditch. Grandpa Smith would take the Red Car (as the Pacific Electric Railway was called) from Los Angeles out to a station just south of their grove.

One day in 1905, there was water running almost to the Red Car station, and as he approached their grove, he realized that it was coming from their land. When he returned home, he told my great-grandmother that if they wanted to have an orange grove, they would have to live on the property.

They built a one-room building with a shed roof, using single-wall construction usually of redwood, which was frequently referred to as California construction. A small room on the west side of the building was called the pantry. It had a kitchen sink with a hand pump, and a pipe from it went to a large cement cistern under the house. The cistern was filled by opening a standpipe out at the road when the grove was being irrigated. There was a linoleum-covered sink top and cupboards along the wall to the right of the sink, and in later years, this room always had an aroma that came from the cookie jar filled with homemade ginger cookies. Every child that ever came there can remember getting a cookie from that jar, which always seemed to be magically refilled.

The one-room house was small, but there was enough room for a bed, table and chairs, and a large wood-burning cook stove in one corner. They later added two bedrooms, a dining room, living room, and a bathroom. They also added a tank house with a windmill that pumped water from the cistern up into the tank. In the house, they removed the hand pump and added plumbing that was more modern.

The ranch—summer kitchen, tank house, and barn are to the left.

The window to the left of the front door is where Grandma Smith would stand and wave good-bye, with tears in her eyes, when we were leaving. Up on the south side of the tank house was a copper solar water heater, which must have been quite an innovation for that time.

Traveling to the ranch, the world seemed to change as we turned off Grand Avenue and onto West Juanita, and ours was the only car traveling through the fragrant, peaceful orange groves. Anticipation grew as we crossed Valley Center Street, and there on the corner was a large plumbago plant that was always covered with beautiful light blue flowers. As we approached the front of the house, we'd see the large jacaranda tree, which in the spring looked like a giant bouquet of blue flowers, but then the flowers dropped and it was like a big fern. Behind it was a large magnolia tree, with its shiny leaves and large pungent white flowers. In the middle of the front yard, a rose-lined walk went from the curb up to the front of the house and then separated to the left and right in both directions to form planters in front of the porch that went clear across the front of the house in typical ranch house fashion. There were always several comfortable rocking chairs where everyone gathered on hot afternoons after working hard in the grove or in the kitchen.

There was an opening in the curb for the long driveway that went up past a large side porch, with steps on three sides, and this is where we entered the summer kitchen. In older houses, it was a rather common thing for family to enter through the kitchen and be welcomed with the wonderful smells of dinner cooking.

The porch outside the summer kitchen was covered with a large grape arbor that extended down past the side of the tank house. I think everyone who came to the ranch toward the end of the summer stood under the vines and picked those beautiful yellow-green seedless grapes from bunches that frequently weighed over thirty pounds. The kids could hardly wait until they got tall enough to reach them for themselves. The wonderful arbor served many purposes besides bearing sweet fruit: it was also beautiful to look at and provided shade for the kitchen in the summer, and then the leaves dropped and let the winter sun warm the room that had glass on three sides.

As we went past the porch, the tank house was next, with just a narrow walk between it and the house, and there was a door that took us back in time when we entered it. There was a damp kind of smell mixing with the fragrances coming from fruits and vegetables stored there. Across the room in one corner was a big square washtub with a hand-operated wringer on one side and a washboard hanging on the wall above it. There were old pieces of furniture stored on the left, such as an old washstand that was no longer needed in the house, with baskets of walnuts sitting on top, waiting to be cracked. On the right was a large fruit cupboard filled with canned jars of peaches, plums, apricots, and many other homegrown crops. There were tall bottles filled with homemade Concord grape juice, and then there were the crocks of watermelon pickles, emitting the fragrance of clove, mixed with other spices.

That homemade grape juice and those pickles were just some of the things that made Thanksgivings at the ranch so special. I will always remember a light with a hook on it that hung on a nail next to the cupboard that had a long cord attached to it so that one could take it and see way to the back of the shelves in the fruit cupboard.

In each corner of the tank house were huge beams that supported the platform way above, on which the tank was situated, and right under the platform, still high up, there was a square insulated tank where the hot water was stored after coming from the copper solar panels on the south side of the building. Over the tank was a roof and then a small platform and above that was the large windmill with its tail that kept it pointed into the wind.

All around the south and west sides of the house, Concord grape arbors kept the single-wall construction house cool in the summer and let the sun warm it in the winter.

Going down the driveway outside the tank house was a fence of Concord grapes and a large satsuma plum tree, and then there was the barn, which in later years was turned into a large two-car garage. The barn was also made from California redwood and was single-wall construction, but the inside walls were left the warm natural redwood rather than being covered with muslin and wallpaper like the house. Way up in the rafters of the garage still hung all the equipment that had been used to hook horses to plows and wagons, and on the east wall was the oiling chart for an early car named Oakland that later took the Pontiac name; that was their first car, bought about 1917. Hanging from nails in the walls were kerosene lanterns and other farm equipment.

To the east of the garage was the chicken coop, and outside it was the typical stump with two nails in it, just far enough apart for the chicken's neck to fit before using the ax to remove its head. In the early days, everyone raised chickens, not only for eggs but for meat as well. As a kid, I never could get over how a chicken would run around with its head off. It seems almost barbaric to think of this today, but it was common then.

In front of the chicken house was a large walnut tree and a persimmon tree. The persimmon tree always lost its leaves around Thanksgiving and displayed those beautiful red-orange fruits that always seemed like a Thanksgiving Christmas tree.

Behind the garage was a roofed shed where all the smudge pots and coke (coal that has been heated to remove the gases and burns very hot) were stored in case of cold weather. These were only needed twice in fifty-eight years, but they were still necessary to have on hand because losing a crop of oranges would probably put them out of business. I think this area was where Garcia, the hired help, slept without heat, cooking, or bathing facilities. Food may have been provided for him, but I am not sure. I know that he was well thought of and was sitting on the back porch crying when Grandpa Smith died.

Although my grandpa Doerr lived on 85th Street in Los Angeles, if it looked as if there would be a freeze, he would go out to the ranch to help his folks in case it was necessary to light the smudge pots throughout the grove.

The laundry was done in the tank house, and across the driveway from it was a large post with arms that could be rotated. Clothes were hung from the wire strung between them (sort of a solar clothes dryer). In later years, this type of clothesline could be bought ready-made. Next to this was a large peach tree, and I remember seeing both grandmothers folding the corners of their aprons to form pouches to carry the ripe, juicy fruit, and we knew we would be getting cobbler for dessert.

At the far eastern boundary of the grove where the irrigation standpipes were, but on the next property, was the Filipino camp, with a two-story barracks-style building and the overseer's house out in front. When I was in high school and college, I spent vacations helping my grandfather work in the grove, and when I was checking the standpipes for water flow, almost before sunrise, there would be men smoking out on the upper porch in their robes. I never saw any women or children, except at the overseer's house. These men probably sent money back to their families in the Philippines.

The overseer had a beautiful early 1930s Packard automobile, and as we sat on the front porch after a hard day's work, he would often drive by and we would wave, but that seemed to be the only acknowledgment for the next-door neighbor. The last time I saw that beautiful car, it was being abused by someone I'm sure was one of his sons. Garcia and Filipinos were the cheap labor for the capitalistic business.

Not only were the sights and smells wonderful at the ranch, but the sounds were gentle and relaxing. The windmill pumping water from the cistern made a rhythmic squeaking-knocking sound, and like the ticking clock in the dining room, it made one feel as though the whole place were alive, and that all was right with the world. Even the out-of-tune whistle of the far-off Pacific Electric Red Car let you know that life was traveling through the beautiful groves.

In 1935, they got gas and were able to have a gas stove and a gas refrigerator. The summer kitchen was not large, but it had windows all around so that there was a wonderful view of orange groves and the tall mountains that were covered with snow in the wintertime. Mount Baldy was one of the most prominent large mountains off to the east, and it was spectacular when shining white with snow. The mountains were always changing colors as the sunlight reflected in different ways. The view from the room was always changing, and one felt as if the view came right into the house. It was easy to see why they had most of their meals in the little summer kitchen.

After Thanksgiving dinners, the kids would play in the grove, getting stung with nettles planted to add nutrients to the soil. Eventually, almost everyone gathered on the front lawn to play and have pictures taken. Some rocked in the chairs on the porch, until it got cool, and then we went in and wound up the old phonograph. We played music and listened to Grandma Smith tell stories about the olden days, even some that her grandparents had told her about sailing between England and the United States. Her grandfather had been a mining engineer and had discovered mines in Pennsylvania, and her mother had been born in Wales while her father was working there.

Toward the end of the day, Grandpa Smith would be sitting in his rocking chair next to the radio, which was up on legs and had doors that he would open before turning on the weather report to see if there were the possibility of frost. The weatherman had a rhythmic, singsongy way of delivery, which always seemed to end in the phrase "and Cucamonga!"—a town east of them.

When it was time to leave, we would say our good-byes on the large back porch, and Grandma Smith would wave as the cars backed out of the driveway. She would then scurry around to the front dining room window and pull the curtains back to wave, always with tears in her eyes, as we started down the street lined with orange groves.

The out-of-tune whistle of the Pacific Electric cars was silenced over a half century ago, and those efficient, clean-running vehicles on tracks were replaced with freeways, covering much more land and carrying polluting trucks, buses, SUVs, and cars. Each time the brakes are applied in one of those vehicles, there is an emission of toxic copper emitted from the brake pads. The change in transportation opened the area to urban sprawl. Those wonderful days at the ranch were nearing an end, and the fragrance of orange blossoms has wilted to only memory.

The wondrous views from the summer kitchen changed from beautiful groves to tract housing, and the mountains were veiled in gray smog. The ranch and all its buildings were replaced with two tract houses, and soon even the memory of those wonderful family times will be gone. The ranch and the gatherings there helped build a strong family and this family left a legacy that helped me overcome my learning disabilities.

The ranch was capitalism at its best and probably what capitalists nowadays think of and wish we could go back to. Self-sufficiency was wonderful, but this way of life was taken over by big business, and small family farms are in the decline, if not nearly gone.

To me, capitalism's negative effects became most evident when capitalism replaced that wonderful clean electric public transportation with private automobiles and freeways that created urban sprawl, with long commutes that kept parents away from their families for longer times. In the 1950's, when visiting Los Angeles, the smog would get so bad that many times I would have to return to San Diego.

Long commute times mean less time spent with family and helping children with homework or just reading to them, but lots of money was made on all those tract houses and building freeways, cars, and buses, all needing rubber tires and so forth.

Los Angeles also had another smog-producing problem and that was that all households and businesses had to burn their own trash. Only wet garbage and cans were picked up for disposal. Anything that could be burned had to be burned on the premises. For the most part, this was the packaging the capitalists used to sell their products. The producers of the trash were not required to be responsible for its disposal; that would be someone else's problem.

Chapter 3

The Farm

My mother's maternal grandfather had grown up in Ohio, and on August 12, 1862, Dru Dryden joined the army and fought in the Civil War until it was over. While in the army on March 15, 1863, he wrote his first letter to Gettie Goss, a childhood friend. After the war, they married and had two children while living in Ohio: Jessie, my grandmother, was born in 1866, followed by Hattie a couple of years later.

President Lincoln had designated Council Bluffs, Iowa, as the place where a railroad bridge should cross the Missouri River, and about nine railroads converged there to cross the river. Dru and Gettie decided to be farmers, and Iowa seemed like a good place, so that is where they went. They found land about ten miles east of Council Bluffs. It had a stream on it so they would not need a well, and that is where they farmed and raised their children: Jessie, Harriet ("Hattie"), Charlotte, Ralph, Cyrus ("Percy"), Gertrude, and Dee.

Jessie, my maternal grandmother, taught school until she was twenty-nine years old, at which time she met William Morris, who was the same age and had taken care of his mother until she died. His father had fought in the Civil War and had died young.

William and Jessie married and started farming just south of where her parents were farming. They had five children: Mildred, Esther, Maxine, Wayne, and Eleanor, my mother. Mildred and Esther were born in a small older house that was on the property when they bought it. This house was torn down and a larger two-story house was moved onto the property.

The farm also had a stream on which they built a small dam, and when it froze in the winter, they cut the ice into cakes and stored it in sawdust in a nearby cave. They would have ice almost all summer, and since Iowa summers are hot enough to hear the corn growing, this was a very refreshing thing to have. They were quite self-sufficient, as they had a large apple orchard just west of the house. They also had chickens for meat and eggs, and cows for milk and cream, which they would take to town to sell for flour and sugar and the few other staples they could not provide for themselves. They would also slaughter farm animals, providing them with dried or canned meat for the long, cold winter.

In the summer, they grew their own vegetables, storing the root vegetables such as carrots, turnips, potatoes, rutabagas, and a variety of squashes in the cellar for winter use. They also stored apples there, making sure they did not touch each other in case one spoiled and spread to the others. This is where the term "bad apple" came from, as one bad apple touching another can make the others go bad. If you associate with rotten people, you will also go bad!

Mother's family on the farm in the apple orchard

Here they raised their five children, Mildred, Esther, Maxine, Wayne, and my mother, Eleanor. It seemed as though my mother, being the youngest, always got the short end of the deal. While her sister Esther was away at Grinnell College, Mom had to walk two miles to the mailbox to get her package of dirty clothes, take them home, wash and iron them, using flatirons on the wood stove, and then package them up to send them back.

To add insult to injury, after Esther graduated from college, she came back to teach in the one-room schoolhouse mother was attending, and Esther would ride the horse to school while Mom walked. Mom would say that Esther was not made to be a teacher, as she would be so engrossed in what she was trying to teach that the boys in the back of the room were doing things she could not even talk about!

Farming behind plow horses was a hard life, but it helped to have neighbors who were there in times of need. The Thomases, their neighbors to the east, were like family, and we are still friends with their grandchildren and great-grandchildren to this day. Mom told the story of the doctor trying to take their eighteen-year-old son's appendix out on the kitchen table. The boy died in the process. This was common in those days because operating conditions were so bad. Even though the patient died, the doctor was probably paid with a ham or some other farm product. I'm sure there was no thought of a lawsuit, so the doctor did not have the enormous liability insurance payments, and he probably had not spent the huge sums it takes for medical school nowadays. There certainly was no need for a national health insurance plan.

I am sure our family was there to help them grieve, and Mrs. Thomas would later come and help my teenage mother take care of her mother when she was dying from cancer. Mom's mother was diagnosed with cancer the day Mom graduated from high school.

Mom spent the next year taking care of her mother, and she said there were times when her mother's sister Gertrude would come out to the farm from Council Bluffs to get butter and eggs and not even go upstairs to see if she could help her sister. Her other sister was the Pottawattamie County superintendent of schools, so she could not help, and because all of her older sisters and her brother had left Iowa by then, that left Mother to do all the work. Grandma died in June of 1929, and then the Depression hit in October. It was not long after that that Grandpa lost the farm and the household furnishings were auctioned off. Living on welfare, he moved to a room in a hotel in Council Bluffs. Even if people had savings in a bank, it was probably gone also, as most of the banks failed.

Aunt Charlotte, mother's aunt had twice been county superintendent of schools in the largest county in Iowa, but after she retired with no pension, she ended up in California on welfare.

These are the good old days that conservatives long to get back to, where everyone was independent and there was no government interference! Farmers did not use chemical fertilizers or pesticides that would need government controls to keep their bad effects from society. Most farming has been taken over by big business capitalists, and the family farmer is about gone. When my grandfather could have used some government help, there was none, but now that faming has been taken over by wealthy conglomerates, there seems to be plenty of government subsidies.

The old farmhouse was torn down long ago and replaced with a manufactured home, as was the Thomas house, but Grandpa's big red barn is still there.

In January of 1930, Mom was standing on the train platform in Omaha in hand-me-down clothes, which included poorly fitting shoes from her aunt Charlotte, with snow blowing around her cold legs and not enough clothes on the rest of her body to keep her warm. She was going to nursing school in Los Angeles, and in those days, hospitals were not only run by churches, but almost all the major churches had their own medical schools.

Chapter 4
Lucille Avenue Reservoir

D ad's maternal grandfather, John Herrnberger, had four brothers and sisters—Frances, Frank, Mary, and Pete—and his parents were both born in Germany. They came to New York in 1848 and then went to Canada, where John was born. They then moved back to the United States, and John was naturalized after his father fought in the Civil War.

As a young man, John moved from Grand Rapids, Michigan, to Detroit, where he was a policeman and a fireman before moving to Los Angeles, where he got a job with the water department; he worked there until his death in 1939.

Dad's maternal grandmother, Jennie Strader, was about fourteen when she came to Los Angeles with her mother and youngest brother on one of the earliest trains coming from Kansas to Los Angeles. This was about 1886, and her father and the older brothers came by covered wagon and met them in Los Angeles. I think it only cost about a dollar by train, and I can't figure out why they didn't all come by train.

They only stayed in Los Angeles for about six years before going to Oregon in the covered wagon. They first went to Medford but found it too hot in the summertime, so they went to Bandon on the coast and homesteaded land. One of the older brothers also homesteaded land, which one of his daughters still lives on now.

By the time they left for Oregon, my great-grandmother Jennie was old enough to marry, and she remained in Los Angeles and married John Herrnberger. They had nine children: Frances, my grandmother (1893), John (1894), Chester (1896), Abbie (1898), Clyde (1900), Fred (1902), Jennie (1905), Conrad (1907), and Frank (1909).

John was not interested in owning property, as the water department always provided a house next to a reservoir that he would manage. The reservoir on Lucille Avenue was where the family gathered often, and always for Christmas.

Grandpa and Grandma Herrnberger

A book could be written about the memorable events that happened at their large family gatherings, but one that was often told was about when my dad was a kid and the boys were chopping wood for the woodstove. My dad got in the way and was hit in the head with an ax. Great-Grandma Herrnberger had been mixing hamburger in a large dishpan, and she ran out with hamburger all over her hands. She was standing over Dad when his mother ("Mom") came running, and seeing all the hamburger on her mother's hands, she thought Dad's brains were running out. She passed out!

My great-grandmother would milk six cows morning and night to earn enough money to buy little houses and fix them up as rentals. She finally admitted in later years that she had bought a neighborhood house and had put a chair on a table to do some painting, and when she was on this makeshift ladder, she felt her fourth child ready to be born. She told my grandmother, Frances, to summon a neighbor as she got down and started for home, but Aunt Abbie was born in the doorway to their bedroom. She said, "I guess I was just made to have babies."

She usually kept her escapades secret from her husband, John, but one day when the boys were teenagers, one of them said at breakfast, "Ma, who's taking care of the gas station today?" When Grandpa heard this, he went through the roof. Not only had she bought a gas station, but she had bought the restaurant next door. She had restaurant supplies under all the tables in the house, and she had put large tablecloths and sheets over them to hide the evidence! She was not only baking pies for the restaurant, but she was doing most of the cooking. When the family got together, which was often, there would be hours of stories like that.

Grandma Herrnberger had put down payments on many small houses, knowing that Los Angeles real estate would be worth something someday, and she had fixed them all up. The rent made the payments—that is, until 1929, when the crash hit and people didn't have jobs to pay rent. All her hard work was lost. However, she was able to keep one property with a little shack on it up in the desert. There was no running water and no electricity, but it was hers, and she liked to spend time there. She always said that you should live near the ocean or in the desert because the air is clean.

One day when I was visiting her in later years, she brought out a large thick pocket watch that had a key to wind it, and the watch had a large gash in it. She said that her grandfather had been wearing the watch while fighting in the Revolutionary War and had been stabbed with a sword; the watch had probably saved his life. One of her oldest great-grandsons has the sword that he had used in the Revolutionary War.

Her husband, John, had worked for over fifty years for the City of Los Angeles and was to get either a small pension or possibly some Social Security, which had recently been enacted, but he died the day before being eligible, and they came and got the check that had already been mailed, leaving Grandma with nothing to live on. She had raised a grandson after his mother's death, and she lived with him for many years, until he remarried, and then she just moved from one of her own children's houses to the next.

Grandma Herrnberger confided in me in later years, I guess because I was about the first in her family to get a college education, and she thought that I would understand better what she was saying. One of these things was that a Catholic priest had molested her husband, Grandpa Herrnberger, when he was an altar boy at ten years of age in 1870. This had a negative effect on his entire life and was the reason we were not Catholic—and why he had not allowed any of his family to attend church.

The other thing she told me, in almost a guilty fashion, was that the only thing she regretted in life was having nine children. She said that she loved each one dearly, but a mother could just not do for nine children what a mother should do. When she died in 1965, all of her children were at her funeral, and I think most of her grandchildren, great-grandchildren, and even most of the eighteen great-great-grand children were as well. She was even written up in the *LA Times* for the number of great-great-grandchildren she had.

Again, these were the good old days that some would like to get back to, when there was a lot of independence but a lot of insecurity.

After Grandpa Herrnberger died in 1939, the Lucille Avenue house was no longer a family gathering place, a place for building a family, and it was soon gone, and family Christmases moved to the 85th Street grandparents' home. The reservoir is now a park ... and the house only a memory.

Chapter 5
Eighty-Fifth Street

A s a young man, my grandfather Harold had many jobs. He was living in San Francisco at the time of the 1906 earthquake but was out of town when it hit. He returned to see the front of his building gone and his bed hanging out of an upper floor!

In 1910, he moved to Los Angeles and was living across the street from the *LA Times* building when it was blown up. Again he was gone, only to return and see the front of his building missing and his bed again hanging out of an upper-floor room.

***Los Angeles Times* building after the bombing**

The abuse as a child had affected him, and he had many jobs, including being a boxer, and he had a failed marriage and was an alcoholic. At some point after the *Times* incident, he went to work as a baker.

His older sister, Cora, had married and had two daughters, Addie and Velma. She abandoned her family when they were young girls, and no one knew where she was for many years. People thought she may have even joined up with Pancho Villa and gone to Mexico. She returned during the Depression with a new husband and three teenage daughters, all needing financial help.

Addie became part of my grandparents' family, and we were always aware of how destructive the abandonment had been to her. In later years, she and her husband, Wesley, would just sit and cry. Nowadays, persons with her background would probably use drugs or alcohol or become addicted to gambling, but not her—outwardly, she was always bubbly and happy, but inside was the pain that came out in tears.

Grandpa's younger sister, Violet, had one son, William, but she and her husband separated, and always lived apart, and it was evident that she had some serious emotional problems, probably having to do with childhood abuse by her father.

Grandpa's father had remarried and had two more boys and a girl, and these children were always close and even came to the ranch, even though they were no relation to Grandpa or Grandma Smith. The youngest of these children was a girl who never married, and when asked in later years how her father had treated her, she said that he had been abusive, and that is why she had never married.

The effects of parental abuse, or abuse by anyone, on children usually causes a lifetime of emotional pain and is then frequently passed on to their children and then their children, generation after generation.

When Frances (my grandmother) was eighteen, she went to work in the same bakery as Harold Doerr, and even though he was older, twenty-five, I think it was love at first sight. I am sure he saw the chance to have the close family that he had not had while he was growing up. She made one stipulation, and that was that he would have to quit drinking if he wanted to marry her.

He quit drinking, and they were married in 1912 and had three children: Harold, my dad (1913), Robert (1918), and Dorothy (1921). This event seemed to have broken the neurotic chain and stopped the abusive behavior that had caused my grandfather's problems, and now he and Grandma would create the family that he had never had.

Pop and Mom's 85th Street house

The year after they were married, they built one of the first houses on 85th Street in Los Angeles, where they raised their children. My grandmother ("Mom"), being the oldest of nine children, loved to cook for large groups, and Sunday dinners were her specialty. Grandpa ("Pop") worked for the telephone company, and even though his days where cut back during the Depression, they still had money for food, and many family members and friends looked forward to Sunday dinners. For some, it was probably the only good meal they got all week. When my dad and his brother, Uncle Bob, were playing local baseball, they would often bring their entire teams home to eat!

While Uncle Bob was playing for the Padres, he lived with Vince and Lena DiMaggio, and then, when the season was over, Vince and Lena lived with Grandpa and Grandma until they could find a place to rent for the off season. Lena taught all the women in the family the "correct Italian way" to make spaghetti and meatballs. During this time, it was common to have many big dinners with upcoming stars like Ted Williams and Joe DiMaggio in attendance. Ted always thought of Pop and Mom as his parents, and they treated him as such.

Vince and Lena were like family as well. They had two daughters, Joanne and Vickie, and I recall asking Joanne, who was about my age, "What does it feel like to have the two most famous people in the world as your aunt and uncle?" At that time, Joe was married to Marilyn Monroe, and she replied, "You know, you're the relative of!" When you are the relative of a famous person you hear the phrase, "Are you the relative of … often. In later years, she mentioned that after her divorce, she had changed her name back to DiMaggio, and she said," I don't think it will get me any more now than it did before!"

My mother arrived in Los Angeles and completed nurses training at the Methodist Hospital. She was working in a hospital when my Dad, Harold, was admitted for an appendectomy. They both were attracted to each other. Their first date was a double date, and they were in the rumble seat of an older car. "Smoke Gets in Your Eyes," and "Deep Purple" were popular songs at the time, and those became their songs. Mother's Methodist minister, Uncle George, husband of her aunt Hattie, married them on October 31, 1934.

Dad and Mother were married about forty-eight years, and when he was in the hospital dying on his last night, mother was holding his hand. She said that every night of their married life, they had held hands before they went to sleep and told each other how much they loved each other. Relationships are so difficult, and it is too bad that not all could be as good as theirs was.

Dad and Mother

When Grandpa Smith died in 1948, my grandparents (Pop and Mom) gave up their home on 85th Street in Los Angeles and moved out to the ranch in order to take care of Great-Grandma Smith and the grove. Death changes families!

Summary

I had a good foundation of families to build from. They were all hardworking and self-sufficient and, with few exceptions, caring and loving. They all seemed to be able to survive adversity, and I cannot ever remember anyone in my family arguing or fighting. I was lucky to have been born into such a wonderful set of relatives.

Part II

My Life

Introduction

Among my varied and unusual life experiences, one included teaching children with learning problems, and I began to examine what the underlying causes for children not learning might be. I then concluded that often the causes can be traced to capitalism; in fact, it may be one of the biggest culprits.

Having taught in the public schools at the junior high and high school levels, I have experienced, observed, and developed ideas and opinions concerning why children don't learn. I feel that some of the causes go back a long way and have been caused by our capitalistic society. I also adopted a six-year-old African American child who had been severely abused before I got him, and who was later diagnosed with ADD, clinical depression, dyslexia, and an eating disorder. I have had to deal firsthand with all these problems, and to this day, I am still trying to help him overcome the abuse and psychological problems that this produced. Hopefully, the chain of destruction will be broken, along with its effect on learning, and his son and my grandson will not be burdened with these problems.

There are several reasons why I want to tell my life story: the first is to show the importance of my family in helping me overcome my learning disabilities, without which I could not have achieved what I have in life.

The other reason is to show that I have life experiences that justify my conclusions as to why children don't learn.

Perhaps the story of how our loving, strong family was built will help others realize that families do not just happen, they must be built with work, caring and togetherness.

Chapter 6

Preschool Years

No one in the family knew that my Dad smoked until I was being born in the hospital and Addie later made the mistake of saying, "Hal said that he had never smoked so much in his whole life." Then the family knew, and I have always wondered if his intake of nicotine before I was born had possibly affected his DNA and caused my reading disability.

1936

My first memory is of being in my father's arms in the original room at the ranch and looking at the big wood cook stove, and this was before I was a year old. Years later, I mentioned this memory and everyone said this was not possible, as that stove was removed when the summer kitchen was added on in 1935, the year I was born. I just said, "How did I know that there had been a cook stove there if I hadn't seen it?"

1937

Dad had been playing minor league baseball for several years, and in the off-season, we would move back to one of the houses next to my grandparents' house on 85th Street in Los Angeles. A couple named Stickley owned these houses; he had been a rumrunner during Prohibition and bought the properties. Alice, his wife, spoke with what I call a New York accent and was always smiling and happy. Around that time, they sold their properties and purchased about two hundred acres a few miles north of Escondido, California, in a rather desolate area that was only reached by rough dirt roads.

Making ice cream

I remember visiting them often in our old Hupmobile, and we would always stop and get a big chunk of ice at the icehouse in Escondido so we could make ice cream in the old-fashioned way with a crank churn. Alice would cook the liquid mixture on the woodstove, using fresh eggs from their chickens and fresh cream from their cow. I could only turn the crank in the beginning, as it got too hard as the process progressed. Salt was added to the ice that had been packed in the churn to make it colder, and you knew it was finally done when you could not turn the crank any longer. It was the best ice cream I have ever tasted. I felt useful having helped turn the crank, even if it was just a little—at almost two years old, it was important to feel needed and useful in the family.

Dad pretty much quit playing baseball and got a job with the telephone company in San Diego. We lived in Chula Vista, a few miles south of San Diego, in a small two-bedroom house. We only lived in the house for six months, and I turned two years old when we moved from there, but I have many memories of things I did there, usually because I was doing things I shouldn't be doing!

Learning about electricity

I remember being in the living room alone, while Mom was busy in the kitchen, and climbing up on the couch. Standing on the arm of the couch, I unscrewed the bulb from the lamp. I pulled the chain and stuck my finger in, only to be knocked down by the electrical shock. Having the curious mind that I have, I got back up and stuck my finger in again, with the same result. Maybe I'm just a slow learner; *in teaching, repetition is a tool used to help children learn!*

Setting the house on fire

Mom's father came from Iowa to stay with us for a while, and he had to use crutches because he had arthritic knees, probably from walking so many years behind a plow. He was supposed to be watching me while Mom was gone. I can remember him sitting in the overstuffed chair with his crutches next to him, and he was asleep. I got the iron out of one of the kitchen cupboards, plugged it in, and set it not far from one of his feet on the living room carpet.

In those days, irons did not have thermostats and would get red hot, and he did not wake up until the iron had burned through the carpet and the padding, and into the hardwood floor, and the room was full of smoke!

Another time I can remember him taking Mom and me to the Safeway store in town, and he stayed in the car to watch me. I was jumping on the front seat next to him and hit my head on the roof. I think that was when I realized that I was growing taller.

Investigating the steam engine

Our house was on Third Street, and the big steam trains would come down the middle of the street, going to the lemon packinghouse just down the street. One day they were oiling one of the big engines in front of our house, and I was with Mom while she was hanging up clothes in the backyard.

She just took her eyes off me for a moment, and I escaped to the front and was right up next to the engine, the steam swirling around me. The engine had a personality all its own; there was the smell of combustion materials, the roar of the flames in the firebox, and the kissing knock of the pump forcing water into the boiler. I was fascinated by the big wheels and all the mechanism out in the open on an external combustion engine.

I would spend the rest of my life fascinated with these machines, but right then, I became aware that the fireman and engineer had turned around and seen me. One of them picked me up and gave me a swat on the backside as he set me on the sidewalk, and Mom was running from the backyard after finding me missing.

In later years, I realized that my interest in mechanical things could be used in my education, because one learns best what one is interested in, and a good teacher can "sneak in" other educational needs using these interests!

I remember so many things that happened when I was two years old. Not only did we move to the San Diego area, but my dad's brother, Bob, who had played baseball for the Hollywood team for two years, was transferred to San Diego when the new Padres baseball team was formed. We spent a lot of time at the old Lane Field and I remember being in the dugout and running through the shower room. I have been told that there was at least one game where Dad was a substitute catcher, Ted Williams was pitcher, and Uncle Bob was second baseman.

Getting hit in the face with a ball
One memorable thing happened before one game, when my Dad had me out on the field. One of his greatest desires was for me to be a successful ball player, so he was trying to play catch with me, but the hardball hit me in the face. This seems like a minor thing, but for a small child, it did psychological damage, as parents are supposed to protect young children from harm. This incident caused me to decide not to be a baseball player.

At these early ages, parents should be careful to protect their children from harm. Sometimes parents tend to think that certain events build character, but they are more likely to cause trauma and problems when they happen at an early age.

Every Saturday, Dad, some of the people he worked with, and I would go to Lane Field to the ball game. After the ball-in-the-face incident, I realized that on one side of the ball park was the train depot, where I could watch steam engines coming and going, and on the other side of the park was San Diego Bay, where there were seaplanes landing and taking off. I started looking forward to Saturdays at the ballpark.

During a game in the Midwest, Dad had watched as his best friend was hit in the head at the plate. He died, and Dad had to accompany his body, on the train, back to Los Angeles. From then on, he was plate shy and had a hard time hitting.

The event that caused pyrophobia

I was a typical two-year-old with lots of energy, and these were Depression times, so one of the only forms of entertainment for my parents was to go to friends' homes to play cards. One evening while they were doing this, I was being so disruptive that the husband of the couple we were visiting picked me up and locked me in the closet with the Murphy bed. I remember hysterically crying, so much so that my folks decided that it was time to go home.

We'd only gone a short distance before we saw fire engines and a big two-story house engulfed in flames. I somehow associated being locked in the closet and the house burning, and to this day, I have a bad case of pyrophobia. As a child, it was even hard for me to sleep in a house with a fireplace. As an adult, I start to pass out at the sight of uncontrolled fires, and if I see smoke ahead on the freeway, I try to exit so I don't cause more problems.

Buying the Rogue River land

At the end of Uncle Bob's season playing with the San Diego Padres, their trainer, Les Cook, and his wife, Blanch, asked him if he would like to spend the off-season with them, fishing on the Rogue River in Oregon. This was a cheap way to live in the off-season with no pay, and he liked to fish, so he went along on a trip that would change his life forever. They went by boat way up the river to Illahe and camped along the river, mostly living off the land.

The area is mountainous and forested, and one day a fellow came out of the woods and asked if they would like to come up for dinner. Well, these folks wanted to sell 160 acres for twenty-two hundred dollars. It was a beautiful place with large butternut trees and a beautiful spring that formed a small pool where pure ice water came up out of the ground, and we would dip in a ladle hanging from one of the trees to get a refreshing drink. This was as close to paradise as the teenage boy Bob Doerr could imagine!

They wanted five hundred down, which Uncle Bob did not have, but he wrote to his dad ("Pop"), who also loved fishing and even tied his own flies, and Grandpa sent him money, changing family life for many years to come.

Uncle Bob went on to the big leagues and was second baseman for the Boston Red Sox for about the next fourteen years, but he was back at the river as soon as each season was over, and this is where he met local teacher Monica Terpin. They were married when he was just twenty years old.

The first family trip to the river in 1939

My next recollections were when I was four years old and we were at my grandparents' house on 85th Street in Los Angeles. We all got up at about four in the morning and drove out to the ranch to pick up Grandpa and Grandma Smith and start our first trip to Oregon.

I remember Dad backing Grandpa Smith's newer Durant automobile out of their garage and putting our Hupmobile in. He began transferring luggage, putting some in a carrier on the running board of Grandpa Doerr's 1935 Chrysler, which didn't have a trunk. Cars were not made for long-distance travel, and trunks were primarily for tools, especially for changing tires.

Crossing the Golden Gate Bridge for the first time

I remember sitting on Grandma Smith's lap in their Durant as we went across the Golden Gate Bridge, and she was telling me about how many men had died building it. That night, we stayed in a motel in Coquille, Oregon, and even though they didn't think there was a railroad nearby, it turned out that the train almost brushed up against the building. In those days, trains seemed to be everywhere, and they seemed to run all night long.

Grandpa Smith took me out the next morning to see the steam engine as the rest of the family packed the cars for the treacherous trip over the mountain on the one-lane logging road that had recently been completed.

It seemed as though the road was too narrow for any kind of traffic, with steep banks up on one side and cliffs into ravines and rivers on the other. The road wound in and out, and each driver would sound his car's horn at each hairpin curve. If you were to meet another vehicle, one would have to back up until there was a wide enough place to pass. It was this way up the mountain and down the other side, until finally there was a little opening in the forest to the right, and a long driveway that went to where the Maples lived. Across from that was a drive that went quite a distance, passing the Whites' little house and continuing down to the river.

Uncle Bob's driveway made a hairpin turn and went back uphill. It was at least a half mile or more to the house, but before you got there, you had to cross a ravine that was bridged only by a large log that had been split long ways, with each half placed at just the width of a car. Small logs on each side kept you from going off, but you came down a hill and had to make a sharp right turn to get onto this bridge. It was always wet and slippery at that turn, and in later years, when that driveway was no longer used, the spring was opened up and the water went to the new cabin.

1939, me, Grandpa Doerr, and Grandpa Smith

1939, Dad with fish

**1939, Mother drinking from the spring
that would soon have stone spillways and waterfalls**

This was all very exciting for a four-year-old, and there would be many learning experiences in self-sufficient living, as the nearest store was at least sixty miles away and there was no electricity.

A fellow named Ellis White had grown up in the forest on the adjoining forty acres, and he and his wife were caretakers for Uncle Bob. They had planted large vegetable gardens, and she would can for the winter. There was fishing every day, and there would be deer meat and, I think, even bear meat. Aunt Monica cooked on a big woodstove that had water pipe coils in it to heat the water, which went up in a tank in the attic to provide hot water. (There also were water pipe coils in the back of the fireplace that did the same thing when there was a fire there.)

Where water comes from
Grandpa Smith took me up into the forest and showed me where the spring water came out of the ground and went into a cement storage box with a pipe that served the caretakers' house, main house, and yard. The big spring near the houses with a ladle hanging from one of the big butternut trees was used for a nice cold drink, but the spring up in the woods provided a gravity feed for the houses and the yard.

Learning by helping the family survive
Aunt Monica made bread in the woodstove about every other day, and being the quintessential teacher, she would always let me help knead it. I felt as though I had truly helped make it, contributing to the family's well-being. She also let me help turn the crank on the churn to make butter.

Grandpa Doerr would milk the cow and put the milk in large pans with lids that fastened to keep animals out, and they would place them in the cold spring water to keep cool. The cream would be so thick on top that if you put it on your morning cereal, you would have to chew it! In later years, I did this, and with the other culinary delights at the river, I gained two pounds a day!

There was so much to be learned there, and it was easy learning with loving family members doing the teaching, but some things you just learned on your own, like touching the chimney of a lighted kerosene lamp and burning a finger. I still have a scar on a finger after touching a smoldering stump. Of course, I had been told not to put my finger in the stump! I remember my younger sister Sharon falling in the icy waters of the spring when she was only a little over a year old. I'm sure that was a learning experience for her!

1939, me

The Maples lived across the logging road and down in a little hollow, and over the years, we got to know them at little parties that the few people living in the wilderness would have for entertainment. Mrs. Maple played the piano by ear, providing the entertainment in her salty way. Mr. Maple had bad sores over his face and body from being gassed in the First World War. In later years, I think Uncle Bob helped him get some pension money and medical help. I remember one time when they went down to San Francisco to the Letterman Army Hospital, and within one day, she had a job as a legal secretary; in later years, it was learned that she had been a secretary to gangster Al Capone! In a way, they were both hiding out in that remote place.

1939, Grandma Smith, me, Grandpa Smith

1939, Grandma Smith and Grandma Doerr ("Mom")

The Schneiders were caretakers at a private lodge across the river, and they had us over there for dinner one evening. Mr. Schneider rowed a boat across to get us and then rowed back across in the dark that night. What an impression that made on a four-year-old, for the Rogue River is known to be fast-moving and treacherous. They say he navigated by the stars.

As we were leaving the river for the first time in 1939, Aunt Monica gave me the little black suitcase containing the windup phonograph, as she would no longer be teaching in the little one-room schoolhouse down in the clearing.

Uncle Bob and Aunt Monica would travel for about the next twelve years, from Oregon to Southern California to visit family, then to Florida for baseball spring training, then to Boston for the baseball season, and then back to Oregon. Their son, Don, was born a few years later, and Aunt Monica would home school him while they were traveling, always thinking like a teacher when seeing something new: *How would I teach that?*

Like the ranch, life on the river was a good example of the times that conservatives long for, with less government and people being responsible for their own survival, conditions that are hard to find nowadays.

In later years, the Schneiders and Uncle Bob bought the Whites' property; the Schneiders bought the four-acre lower corner near the river, and Uncle Bob bought the thirty-six acres that were higher up and featured a beautiful view of the river. The Schneiders built what is now called the Illahe Lodge, and it is still owned by their grandson.

They sold the original property and built on the new property, which had easier access to the logging road, as well as to the river and the view. They built this new place in about 1960, and the family was welcomed there from then on. The new place had electricity, which made life much different, and they even had a dishwasher. There were windows all across the front, looking out toward the mountains and the river. Many evenings, we all sat and watched the full moon come up over the mountains and cast a shimmer across the river below. There was a large deck outside the windows, where the family would sit in the afternoons and watch the colorful hummingbirds come to the feeder, and we could also see who was fishing on the river. The deck was also where the whole family would gather to take a family picture just before leaving the river.

My first train trip

In 1939, we lost Grandpa Morris, my maternal grandfather. Mom, her older unmarried sister Esther, my sister Sharon, and I were going to take the train back to Council Bluffs, Iowa, for his funeral. I remember what a time Mom had trying to find disposable diapers for Sharon, something almost unheard of in 1939.

We left on the train from the new station in Los Angeles, which was the last of the palatial stations to be built, and its grandeur and beauty remain today. Having to sleep with Aunt Esther in the upper berth was the most memorable part of the trip, and I'm sure it was for her too; she had been a teacher for a short time and learned early that children were not her thing.

While there for the funeral, we stayed with Aunt Maxine, another of Mom's older sisters, and her husband, Ray, seemed to be in charge of keeping me occupied with taking out a stump in the front yard. The day of Grandpa's funeral, I remember everyone getting in the car, and I wanted to go, but Uncle Ray convinced me to stay.

After the funeral, Aunt Maxine brought out a shoebox filled with IOUs, showing that Grandpa had lent money to many of his neighbors, money that had never been repaid, yet they had all been there taking furniture while the farm was foreclosed on.

We all then went out to what had been my great-grandfather's farm, ten miles east of town. The farm now belonged to one of his sons. We had dinner, and then I remember playing in the yard with other cousins.

The next day, we were invited to the Thomases' for dinner. It had been raining, and the dirt farm roads were slick, but Aunt Maxine thought she could make it, as that was where she had learned to drive. We turned off the main paved highway and onto the farm road. I was in the backseat with Mother and Sharon, and the back of the car made a violent swing to the left and then to the right, and we ended up down in the ditch. Aunt Max managed to do a little rocking back and forth and, using just a little gas, got us out.

We made it to the Thomases', who had been their next-door neighbors growing up, and after seeing all their livestock, we had a wonderful dinner with people whose grand-children and great-grandchildren we still consider family.

Chapter 7

My School Years

I could write a book just about kindergarten, but suffice it to say that I heard the teacher died after that year! I do remember one incident where my friend Danny and I were walking home from school, and as we walked through a vacant lot less than a block from our houses, there was a solid fence on one side, I threw a large rock over the fence and there was a large splash. This was fun for a five-year-old so I threw several more! That afternoon, a woman appeared at our front door, demanding that my mother pay for her goldfish that had been killed with the rocks!

Dad only made sixty-four dollars a month, and they paid thirty-four dollars in rent, which left only thirty-four dollars for four people to live on, and these fish were not even edible. Dad got paid every two weeks, so Mom would pay seventeen dollars of the rent every two weeks so we had a roof over our heads. She always made sure she had a dime to buy a day-old loaf of bread for five cents and a head of cabbage for five cents, and that is what the four of use ate for a couple of days before each payday. My grandfather had bought us a used refrigerator, but most of our neighbors still had iceboxes, and we kids looked forward to the ice man coming because he would usually chip off a small piece of ice for each of us to suck on, and we thought that was a great treat. He also knew that if we were sucking on the ice, we would be less likely to hitch a ride on the back of his truck as he drove along. We had a telephone because my dad worked for the phone company and had to be called out if there was an emergency, but most of our neighbors did not have one.

My friend Danny lived with his mother and older brother across the street from us, in a court next to his great aunt and uncle. He couldn't say his great aunt's name, which was Gracie, so he called her "Dadee," and that is what she went by the rest of her life. Dadee and her husband, Roy, had a small two-bedroom house, and they slept in the front bedroom. Her elderly deaf aunt slept on the small enclosed front porch, with just enough room to walk by her bed to get to the house. Her mother slept on the couch in the living room, and her sister slept on a daybed in the dining room.

I remember Danny's mother having asthma and using a spray as she tried to breathe. She died one night, and Dadee and Roy took in Danny, who was four years old at the time, and his brother, Frank, who was about fourteen. They had a bunk bed in the small back bedroom. Dadee took care of her aunt, her mother, her sister, and her husband, Roy, until they died, and one of her greatest losses was Danny, whom she thought of and loved as her own son, who died of a stroke at about forty years of age. Dadee lived into her mid-nineties, and if ever there was a saint, it was her.

Again, these were the good old days that some would like to go back to, with no Social Security or any government help when there was no work, people who would take in other family members and even friends.

We lived near the avenue with streetcars, and on the corner was a skating rink, where they had one of the new Hammond B3 organs that we could hear into the night, and I would usually fall asleep to this kind of music. I was in a comfortable, protected atmosphere and being lulled to sleep with music was probably one of the factors in my enjoyment of music to this day. We didn't have a radio or phonograph, and neither did our neighbors at that time, so music was quite special, even if it did come from a distance.

A month into first grade, we moved to La Mesa, a town about ten miles east of San Diego, and it seemed as though I was behind everyone in my new class. I had a reading problem that I call a form of dyslexia, and little was known about it in those days. I could only recognize one letter at a time, and that happened slowly. The part of my brain that processes reading just had not developed.

I was kept in the second grade for two years. I don't think that really did much good, and it was hard on me psychologically.

December 7, 1941, and the war years

December 7, 1941, my sister Sharon and I were in our 1939 Plymouth while my dad was washing it before church. I had turned on the radio in the car, and in those days of tube radios, they ran the battery down fast. Dad turned the water off and heard the radio. He hollered to turn it off, and I did just as it was announced that Pearl Harbor was being attacked, and then he stared yelling, "Turn it on, turn, it on!" Dad was called to work that afternoon to start wiring the leftover fair buildings in Balboa Park so they could be used for offices and hospitals.

One of the events that probably changed my life more than anything else happened at a Cub Scout meeting held at the den mother's house. Our activities were outside, and it began to rain, so she took us into a little house in the avocado grove. There was what looked like an upright piano, but it was a player organ, and she began playing "Hail, Hail, the Gang's All Here" on the manual keys. I was looking at the boxed rolls sitting on top, and when she finished playing, I asked her what they were, and what roll did she pick to play but the "William Tell Overture." I had heard the fourth movement many times as the theme music to the radio program "The Lone Ranger," but I had never heard the first three, dealing with the storm, which was especially appropriate on a stormy day. In later years, this player organ and the approximately 275 rolls of music would be stored at our house—in fact, in my bedroom. When it needed repairs, I worked on it.

This began a lifelong love affair with organs, both player and pipe organs. Mom took me to my first organ concert when I was six years old, and it was at the First Methodist Church in San Diego, which had a large pipe organ. The famous organist Richard Elsasser played and I still remember it. Many years later, I would help take this pipe organ out of that building and move it to their new location.

One day I was on my bicycle, going to a scout meeting, and when I stopped at a stop sign next to a car with a radio on, it was announced that President Roosevelt had died. Everyone was shocked when I got to the meeting and told them.

My grandparents lived in Los Angeles, so we would go between San Diego and their house on 85th Street in Los Angeles about every other week, and we went to Oregon many times as well. There was always popular music on the car radio, which I associated with the wonderful times of family being together.

Thanksgiving during the war years
One Thanksgiving during WWII, Grandpa and Wesley (Addie's husband) had to work for the telephone company. Thanksgiving, as usual, was planned for the ranch. Dad, Mother, Grandma, Sharon, Addie, and I would go out there in Grandpa's 1935 Chrysler. Grandpa and Wesley would come to the ranch after work.

There were no freeways in those days, so it was quite a trip, going through small towns, and making many turns on to new and different terrain. After going through El Monte, there was a long bridge over a dry riverbed and then a left turn over several railroad tracks. The first track was quite a jolt, and the car stopped dead on the next track. There was a steam locomotive whistling, getting ready to leave the station a short distance down the track.

With his right foot, Dad kept shoving on the starter, which was a large pedal on the fire wall in those days, with no results. Addie grabbed me and said, "Come on, Hallie, we've got to push." I was called Hallie because there were three Harolds in our family and Aunt Dot had married into a family of Harolds. Everyone started to get out of the car. About the time we all started to push, someone realized that the car key was on the dash over on the passenger side. Grandma's knee had hit it and turned it off when we bumped over the first track. It was another wonderful family memory as we all pushed together, and I felt very important trying to push the car off the tracks and out of danger as the steam engine was sounding its whistle and starting to move on its way toward us.

Time with my grandfather and a sense of belonging to family

Another event involving a car happened on a Sunday during WWII. Uncle Bob's family and ours had just finished dinner at 85th Street, and it was school vacation time. I would be spending time with my grandparents. We finished one of Grandma's big dinners, and then Uncle Bob's family left to go back to Camp Roberts (he was in the army). My family had departed for La Mesa.

Grandma had already finished cleaning up after dinner and was crying in the bedroom as she always did after saying good-byes to her children. The phone rang, and it was Uncle Bob, saying that the LaSalle had overheated on the steep mountain roads going over the Sepulveda Pass to the San Fernando Valley. They were at the bottom of the mountain in the San Fernando Valley, and he knew that the car could not make it over the steep Ridge Route Mountains to Bakersfield and then more mountains on the way west to Paso Robles. He asked Grandpa to bring the Chrysler and pick up the LaSalle.

Grandpa hollered, "Come on, Hallie! We gotta go!" We hopped into the Chrysler, and Pop and I headed west on Manchester to Sepulveda and then north up the mountain and through the tunnel down to the other side to help get the family out of a jam.

**Aunt Monica, Uncle Bob,
and son, Don, in front of the LaSalle**

There the three of them were, standing alongside the LaSalle, with a row of eucalyptus trees and a citrus grove on the other side of them. This was about where the 101 and the 405 freeways cross now, but in those days, it was all narrow two-lane roads. We got their bags transferred, and they were on their way to Camp Roberts, and Grandpa and I were together as he slowly maneuvered the LaSalle on Riverside Drive, which went around the mountains, and then on to Figueroa and back to 85th Street.

Those times with my grandfather were wonderful and memorable, as he always had life-changing sayings that he would impart such as: "If you meet your wife in a bar, you're going to keep going back there to find her!" I think this is the time he told me about living in San Francisco at the time of the earthquake—and across from the *Times* building when it was blown up. Grandpa had only a grade school education, but he was one of the most intelligent, knowledgeable men I have ever known.

It was around that time that Grandpa taught me how to tie fishing flies, and I'm sure that while he was doing so, he was dreaming of using them on the Rogue River in Oregon. Back then, radios were up on legs with doors on the front, and he had taken one of those and removed the radio and inserted shelves for his jars of feathers, containers of hooks, and other makings for flies, and there was a slide-out shelf for the vice that held the hook while you assembled the fly. I still have the flies that he guided my hands to make, and every time I see them, I remember that day he taught me to make them.

Frequently at family gatherings we would go out in the yard and take pictures. The one of my sister Sharon and my cousin Virginia with me was memorable because Sharon would die at the age of fifty from ovarian cancer, and Virginia would die at ten from asthma.

After WWII our family was able to resume traveling to Oregon from Southern California and my mother's oldest sister Mildred and her husband Earnest and son Loren had moved to Redding California. Redding was about half way and a good stopping place. In the summer of 1947 Lena DiMaggio, Joanne, Vicky, and a friend of hers arrived at the 85th St. house where my family and grandpa and grandma were ready to leave for Oregon. The DiMaggio family would only go as far as Sacramento where Vince was playing ball, but the rest of us would go on to stay a few days in Redding.

Uncle Ernest had worked building Shasta Dam and was able to arrange a tour through the dam and power house. I was only twelve years old so this was very exciting and we even got to go in to the penstocks, the big pipes that provide the water to turn the generators.

In 1949 on our trip we stopped in Redding then the Rogue River, then over to Bandon on the coast where Grandma Herrnberger was living with her grandson. We then went over to eastern Oregon to Uncle Wayne's home for a reunion of mother's family. Uncle Wayne was able to arrange a tour through the sugar factory where he worked and where sugar beets were made into sugar.

The rout from eastern Oregon to southern California is mostly through desert that is hot in the summer time and our '47 Chevy got vapor lock several times. This is where the gasoline going to the engine turns to vapor and the gas pump can only pump liquid, so there is a wait for the gasoline to cool and return to a liquid before the engine will run again.

I also remember that one of the popular songs we heard often on the car radio on that trip was *At Last* and this was the music that, sixty years later, President and Mrs. Obama danced to at all of their inaugural balls.

Sister Sharon, me, and Cousin Virginia

Another family time I remember during the war was when Dad's second cousin, who was half American Indian and stationed with the navy in San Diego, would come and have Sunday dinner with us. He was about ten years older than I, but still a teenager, and I remember him as a good person who was fun to be around, and our neighbors would always mention what a handsome guy he was in his navy uniform. After the war, we would see him in Oregon where he lived, and getting to know him probably help form my positive image of Native Americans.

One thing that did make a difference in my reading in elementary school was that if I were given subject matter that I was especially interested in, like helicopters, new to us after the Second World War, I would make the effort to read, albeit slowly. This happened in the fifth grade, and I thought the teacher was going to cry. I wasn't being forced to read boring Dick and Jane—but finally something that was interesting.

My folks had gotten tutors for me and done everything they could, and I learned that I just had to work much harder than other children did in order to read and learn.

I grew out of my discipline problems, and at the end of sixth grade, I was awarded a two-week all-expenses-paid vacation to Catalina Island for good citizenship. Three other boys from other schools were also given this award, and along with a wonderful married couple chaperoning us, we had a great time. The wife had been a theater organist before the Depression, when all women organists were let go. She said she then went into nursing because that was something men did not do in those days. She and I spent a lot of time in the theater at the casino, where there was a pipe organ and regular concerts. Mom, Dad, Addie, Raymond, Lena DiMaggio, and Joanne all came to visit while I was there.

My first airplane ride

We had never seen Uncle Bob play ball while in the major leagues, and in the summer of 1950, the day after the Korean War started, we left San Diego at about nine in the evening on a small two-engine plane that sat at such a slant that you could hardy walk up the aisle. We changed to a four-engine plane in Los Angeles, leaving there at about eleven o'clock.

We got to Chicago at about seven the next morning and refueled. We stopped in Cleveland and Hartford, Connecticut, and then we finally arrived in Boston at about two thirty in the afternoon. This was the fastest flight at that time! The plane had noisy piston-driven engines and was not pressurized, so we never got more than ten thousand feet high. I spent the whole night looking out the window at the land below, with headlights of cars making their way on narrow roads, usually through farmland.

On August 2, 1947, the Red Sox had a day honoring Uncle Bob and had given him a lot of gifts; among them was a new 1947 Cadillac. The afternoon we arrived at Uncle Bob's in Boston, our new sea-green 1950 Mercury was delivered; that was on June 27, 1950 and I don't know which I enjoyed riding in more, our new 1950 Mercury or that 1947 Cadillac.

We got to see Uncle Bob play in many games, and when Uncle Bob was playing out of town, Aunt Monica took us to see all the historical things near Boston, such as the Old Manse, Walden Pond, the House of Seven Gables, and Bunker Hill, just to name a few.

We also saw the statue of the minuteman at Lexington and the one of the Fighting Farmer at Concord. I am sure that the framers of our Constitution were referring to these people when they put the phrase "being necessary for a regulated militia" in the Constitution, and that these men realized that when they picked up arms, they were regulated by the military. The gun toters and minutemen of today want no controls, and I'm sure that if the framers of the Constitution could see how guns have changed, they would probably outlaw them all. Nowadays, there are military contractors carrying guns, and I have a feeling that they do not consider themselves a well-regulated militia, not properly under the control of the military.

During my years of teaching, I have had students and the family members of students killed with guns, and I have never been able to think of anything good that can be done with a gun.

Minute Man Monument, Concord, Mass.
Dedicated in 1875. Daniel Chester French, Sculptor.

Statues of the minuteman and the Fighting Farmer

It was interesting to be with a famous person who didn't have to pay for all of us in any restaurant; he just signed autographs for the restaurant workers, and many times the owner would come and sit with us.

The Red Sox then played down in New York and we had driven from Boston down there, and after sightseeing in the city, we went to see them play at Yankee Stadium. We left the ball game that evening and started on our way back to the West Coast.

It took six days of driving on two-lane roads so narrow that you had to go off in the mud when passing trucks, but we got to Aunt Maxine's, in Council Bluffs, on my fifteenth birthday, which I had forgotten, but she had dinner and a birthday cake ready when we arrived.

The Spreckels Pipe Organ
The first place I drove after getting my driver's license was to the Spreckels Organ Pavilion in Balboa Park in San Diego, as my interest in pipe organs had just kept growing. In 1988, I was a founding member and first vice

president of an organization we called SOS—for Spreckels Organ Society. There had always been Monday evening summer programs presented by our civic organist, but it was decided that it would be nice to have a summer organ festival and bring organists from all over the world. These programs vary from all Bach to light theater and jazz organ and each year a silent movie night, and we usually have two to four thousand attending each program.

The organization also tries to promote young student organists, showcasing them on Sunday programs, and in conjunction with the local Guild of Organists, gives scholarships to encourage them.

The organization developed a program where fifth graders come to the park on Fridays and sit on the stage around the organ console while an organist presents a short program suitable for their age. SOS commissioned a piece of music called "Rex the King of Instruments," which has dialogue to accompany it, describing how the organ works.

There are many fund-raisers, and one of the most popular is also educational. After a nice brunch at a nearby restaurant, we walk over to the Pavilion and sit on stage for a short concert and an explanation by the organ curator of how the organ works. Then we take the whole group through air locks in the organ wind chest so they can see how all the mechanism works while the organ is being played.

One of the most moving events for me was when we had about a dozen deaf students come to "hear" the organ, which truly was a feeling event. They all had balloons, and I took them upstairs, where they could look in at the big pedal pipes of the organ while it was being played and actually feel the music through the balloons and see the panels of the doors vibrating as the large pipes sounded. They would put their hands on the door panels going into the organ chambers, (you can actually see the door panels going in and out) and they could feel the music. They all were so excited that they wanted me to hold their balloons so that I might "feel" the music!

My high school years

The most memorable thing from my high school years was during my sophomore year, when my ten-year-old cousin, Aunt Dot's daughter, Virginia, died suddenly during an asthma attack. My Aunt Dorothy,

Dad's sister, had spent a great deal of time trying to find a place where her little girl, Virginia, could breathe, and with her husband Stan away in the war, moving to the desert had been a difficult decision.

She found that Virginia could breathe best up in the high desert at Twentynine Palms, California, with its warm, dry air, and it was far enough away from the extremely polluted air of Los Angeles. There were few people living there then, and if I remember correctly, the first time I was there in 1944, the *tupuck, tupuck* of the electric generator stopped at about nine in the evening, and there was no electricity in town after that.

Escaping the polluted air of Los Angeles was a big help, but so many people smoked in those days that the air was almost always polluted with cigarette smoke. With WWII came the draft, and almost all men went into the service, where along with the food rations came free cigarettes, and since all your buddies were blowing smoke at you, you usually took up the habit too. The tobacco industry knew that nicotine was addictive, and once they got you hooked they would likely have you for life, and when Uncle Stan, Virginia's father, came home from the war, she was breathing in even more secondhand smoke.

We know that nicotine has an effect on brain cells, but all cells in the body are being bathed in this chemical, even the reproductive cells, and DNA could even be affected for future generations. With her allergy to air pollutants, Virginia didn't have a chance. We see an increased incidence of asthma today, and even if we want to deny global warming, we should be concerned about how pollutants are affecting our bodies and our children's learning.

Virginia often went to catechism with one of her friends after school, and one day she came home and said that the lesson that day had been about a little boy who had died and gone to heaven. While in heaven, he watched over and prayed for his loved ones back on Earth. It was just a few days after this that the little girl's mother called Aunt Dot and said that a mutual friend was coming over that afternoon, and that she should come over and visit. My aunt said she had to do ironing, but the mother succeeded in convincing her to come over and do her ironing while they visited.

They picked up the girls from school, and they were visiting and Aunt Dot was ironing clothes while the girls played. It was common for Virginia to come ask her mother for the spray that would help her breathe, but the response was slow that day, and finally Aunt Dot realized that they needed to get her to the hospital. Aunt Dot was driving, the friend was holding Virginia in the front passenger seat, and the others were in the backseat.

Suddenly, the friend started shaking Virginia because she had stopped breathing, and nothing they did at the hospital helped. Aunt Dot and her family turned to religion to deal with this grief, and it was there for her when she lost three children, two husbands, and many other loved ones.

Virginia's funeral was on the following Sunday in a small church there in the desert, and the entire family was there, many packed in a small room at the back of the sanctuary. It was time for the family viewing, and Uncle Bob was on one side of Grandma, and my dad was on the other. I was directly behind them, with Addie at my side. As they approached the coffin and Grandma saw her lifeless little curly-haired angel, she lunged out of her son's arms and instinctively reached to pick her up, at the same time letting out screams of grief and then passing out.

I had never seen anything like this, and thinking she was dying, I began to cry and repeat, "She's dying, she's dying." Addie put her arms around me and kept saying, "She'll be all right." A doctor was summoned and gave her a shot. This was how I learned about grief.

Addie and her son, Raymond, would only live another five years or so. Ray was diagnosed with terminal cancer at thirty years old, and Addie was sitting by his bedside one evening and slumped over. She was taken to the hospital, and she died a few hours later of a cerebral hemorrhage. Ray died four weeks to the day later. It almost seemed as though she died of a broken heart when she realized that she was losing her only child; she hadn't had a mother when she needed one the most, and now she was losing another love of her life.

The evening after Virginia's funeral, we headed back to the ranch. I was driving our car with my mother, Dad was driving Grandpa's car in back, and ahead of me was Uncle Bob, driving their 1950 Cadillac. Beside him in the front was Aunt Monica, and I could just see the tops of Grandpa's and Grandma's heads through the back window. I could see that they were in a loving embrace, having just lost one of their most cherished possessions.

As I drove along, the whole car ahead radiated grief, and our car radio seemed to keep repeating the song "Delecado." Whenever that music plays, I always have bittersweet memories of a wonderful family gathering for such a grief-filled occasion. Now when I relive this event, "Adagio for Strings" by Samuel Barber runs through my mind, and my eyes still fill with tears. This was the music used so effectively in the movie *Platoon* to impart the enormous feeling of grief that accompanies the emotions of war.

When I returned to school, my admit card read "Death in family," and my English teacher, who had asthma herself, asked who it was. I told her, and she asked me to come in at lunchtime, which I did, and she helped me write a poem about my loss.

This is an example of an excellent teacher recognizing a teaching moment.

Many years later, I would speak at her memorial service and express my gratitude for having had such a wonderful person in my life. These are the words Shakespeare used when dealing with death: "When he shall die, take him and cut him out in little stars, and he will make the face of heaven so fine that all the world will be in love with night and pay no worship to the garish sun."

Eleanor Roosevelt made this statement: "No one can imagine this earth without them on it." This causes me to think about my own mortality.

Psalm 23 brings a great deal of comfort to many.

When my youngest sister, Janet, started college, my mother decided to go back to work nursing and she was hired at our county geriatric nursing home. She worked the evening shift and there were typically only two nurses for about five hundred patients at night. She saw an average of two deaths per night.

Several years after she retired, a call came that her oldest sister, Mildred, was not expected to live after fighting cancer for several years. She and Dad left immediately to be with her, and when my mother, who had taken care of so many people while they died, saw her sister, she said that she would not be alive in the morning. Mother helped take care of her for about nine more months. The moral of the story is that no one knows for sure how long you are going to live, not even your doctor or your nurse.

Recently, a colleague of mine and I attended the memorial service for one of our fellow teachers who happened to be a drama teacher. The participants had a captive audience for over two hours.

After about two hours, my friend's cell phone went off full blast, thereby stopping the service, and it took him a bit of time to get it turned off. It was not five minutes later that it did it again, stopping the service a second time, and then a few minutes later, the phone went off on full volume, stopping the service a third time. Someone said, "I think Art [the deceased] is trying to tell us something!"

Then the back legs of my chair collapsed with a loud bang, and I went backward; my legs were in the air, and my head was in the lap of the woman behind me. I could not get up, and most everyone there was elderly, so it took a while to find someone young enough to extract me from the chair. The service resumed, only to be interrupted a few minutes later by a jackhammer right outside the building. My friend and I left as quickly as possible, forgoing the reception.

A few days later, we had a family gathering before going to my grandniece's Christmas play, and I was telling the preceding story to the family while they worked in the kitchen. Then I went into the family room and sat on the couch near my six-year-old grandnephew. Evidently, he had heard me telling the story about the memorial service problems. Unexpectedly, he looked at me with a sad face and said, "What did you do with Grandma [my mother] after she died?"

I am not a fast thinker, but I learned years ago that when all else fails, tell the truth, and in this case, I tried not to dramatize or be too blunt. I told him that Great-Grandpa (my dad and Grandma's husband) had died many years ago, and that when people die, they no longer need their bodies so we have cemeteries where we put their bodies in the ground. I told him that we put Grandpa in one and left a space for Grandma, and that his grandma (my sister Sharon, who had died) had been buried in the next space. Great-Grandma was now between her husband and her daughter (his grandma).

It had never dawned on me that we had left the younger children with a sitter at my niece's home, where the reception was to be held after Mom's services, and that now their loving great-grandmother (they had never known their grandmother, my sister) was just gone without any explanation. I also realized how devastating it is for a child, who has a limited concept of death, to begin to understand what has happened.

When dealing with death in the school setting, I had students come into my office just to cry, and I would ask them, "Would you like me to stay or leave?" They would let me know how much pain they were feeling, and sometimes they would just like to talk. I always gave each one a list of others to get help from, beginning with his or her church, as many churches have good grief counseling, and there were also counselors and teachers that the student could go to.

Over the twenty-five years that I had my little office hidden away in the back of the career center, not only did students come to cry, but even some teachers and administrators. They also came when there was a divorce in the family, which is almost the same as a death. Everyone seemed to know that my office was a place where they could come and be alone in their grief, and that I was understanding and sometimes even helped them cry.

There was a study done of a large number of people that lived to be over one hundred yeas old, and they all had four things in common. What is interesting is that one would think they all had good diets. Quite the contrary; none seemed to have had a good diet! Two of the things they had in common were that they all had something to look forward to each day, and they all had some way of dealing with loss.

We are able to help people deal with this area of psychological pain, but it still has a great effect on all of our lives, and on children's learning, until the healing process takes place.

Grossmont High School was filled with extremes, and I remember one student, who came from a wealthy family, driving his new Cadillac convertible to the bus stop so that he could ride the school bus with the rest of us. The Indian students would come in from the reservations, where they had very few material things, and perhaps sit next to the student who drove the Cadillac to the bus stop.

Over the years, three future astronauts would attend this high school: Rick Sturckow, Ellen Ochoa, and Bill Anders. To date, this is probably the most astronauts to attend any one high school.

An example of good teaching

Good teachers make learning as interesting as possible with the realization that each student comes to them with a different set of interests and aptitudes, and that using these interests or introducing them to new subjects that may interest them will let the student learn easier, faster, and better. Learning takes place better when students can apply what you want them to learn by doing an exercise using their special interests.

I will now share an example of good teaching. When I was a junior in high school, my English teacher made an assignment to give a speech on how something worked. The topic I was interested in at that time was automobile automatic transmissions, so I went to the local auto dealer and got many pictures of the internal workings of an automatic transmission to use as props.

In my speech, I showed the class how the engine was disconnected from the wheels by a fluid coupling; the part connected to the engine acted like a fan and the part connected to the wheels acted like a windmill. These two mechanisms were all in oil instead of air.

Then I explained how gears were changed using a planetary gear set (also used on the old model T Fords), and how it was made up of three parts: the sun gear, the planetary gears, and the ring gear. From each planetary gear set, you can get two forward speeds and one reverse just by stopping one of the components with a band or clutch. Today's automatic transmissions are similar but more complicated.

The English teacher gave a general assignment, but let the students choose the subject, knowing that they would work hard and even do a better job writing if they were interested in the subject.

An example of bad teaching

I was on the new *QE2* ship a couple of years ago, and a beginning class in computers was offered. I knew I needed to know the basics at least, so I attended. Each person in the class had a computer in front of him or her, which could easily have been practiced on, but the teacher, or non-teacher, talked for a whole hour, explaining some things but never letting us use the computers to practice. No learning took place.

In the above example, the teacher should have given a basic explanation of how computers work and what they can do for us, and then he should have shown how a computer is turned on, letting us turn ours on. Then he should have given us a lesson on how the mouse works, the tasks it performs, and what left and right clicks do, as well as double clicks, and in each case, let us perform that function so that we could actually understand and commit the process to memory.

I hope these examples will help you understand the teacher-learning process, if you were not already aware of it.

Positive gangs

Educators had it right many years ago when they provided something for everyone to come to school for. The students essentially formed "positive gangs" with other students who had similar interests. There was a wide range of subjects, activities, clubs, and after-school activities forming the nucleus for these positive gangs.

In the communities, there were other positive gangs run by the Boy Scouts, Girl Scouts, YMCAs, churches, and the list could go on and on. These gangs provided a sense of belonging in many aspects of the community, and there was at least one place in society where each child could find success and a sense of belonging.

The attitude now is to fail them, and many failures in their lives could be why they are not learning. It would be much more productive to find a place for them where they could succeed and be productive. The variety of subjects and activities has been curtailed lately in the name of economy, but the effect on society has been much more expensive.

When I was young, our church had several positive gangs that I belonged to. There was a group of us who ushered every Sunday, and I did this for five years. It made us all feel as if we were a more important part of this organization.

I also went in during the week and set up the church marquee that announced what the sermon would be for the next Sunday. I was active in the church youth groups that met on Sunday evenings, and we frequently went to different homes afterward for social get-togethers and refreshments. We also had retreats at the church camp, as well as dances and beach parties. This positive gang still gets together, even after more than fifty years—unfortunately, sometimes for memorial services.

This church also had a program where several groups of high school students, with adult male and female counselors, would travel from Southern California during the Easter week and work on Native American churches in Arizona. We learned the importance of organizing to prepare food to feed the group. We also learned to have the supplies and be organized to complete a job.

The Indian children frequently worked with us, giving us a wonderful opportunity to get to know people that we would probably never meet otherwise. The young people on these work teams came away not only with new close friends from home but knowledge about people that have been misrepresented in our society for too long. They came away with loving, caring relationships with people that they had considered "different," and perhaps inferior.

Having a sense of belonging is important

Most importantly, activities of this nature give the participants a sense of belonging. If a child is not succeeding academically, some other productive activity should be found for them so they don't leave school and form "negative gangs."

There are seventeen Indian reservations in San Diego County, and at the time I attended high school, Grossmont High was the closest high school to several of them. I realize now that many Indians had started high school, and I would see them, but I assumed they were Mexicans, as I didn't know there were Indian reservations near by.

As I look through old annuals, I realize that none seemed to have graduated, and later I began to learn how different their lives must have been, and how hard it must have been for them to attend that school.

My college years

When you don't see words, your spelling and reading skills are going to be bad. Therefore, I went to a reading lab in college, where I worked with tachistoscopes, which flashed numbers on a screen and kept adding more in order to widen my field of vision. This helped, but reading was still slow, and I could never learn to read music, as the lines were just an added confusion. Comic books almost caused a short circuit in my brain, as there was just too much going on for my brain to decipher.

I ended up majoring in industrial arts, where there was less reading, and my most difficult subject was history, as it took me probably five times longer to read than the average student. I had learned early on that if I wanted to get any place, I would just have to work harder than others did, especially because I had decided to go into teaching. I felt that using Cliffs Notes would be cheating, but I should have been told to use them, for at least I would have gotten an overview of things like history, which would have been better for me than spending the amount of time it took me to read.

I also thought that I had to do all the work myself, and I never had anyone correct spelling or proofread my papers. I always did my own typing as well. That may have made me a better person, but it was sure hard at the time, and my grades were not as good as they might have been.

Thinking it would be practical, I made the mistake of getting a job in the school library. I took library science classes and got the job, which paid fifty cents an hour. This seemed good after receiving fifteen cents a pair for shining shoes in the local barbershop at twelve years old—and thirty-five cents per hour for babysitting and yard work before that. Nights and weekends in the library were dark and depressing.

In my junior year, I took the state test to become a driving instructor and started making two dollars an hour at a private driving school. Because I had patience, they always gave me the difficult students. In those days, they were frequently nurses and older people who needed to learn to parallel park to renew their licenses.

Two weeks after graduating from college, I was drafted into the army.

Chapter 8

My Army Years

I went through basic training at Fort Ord, near Monterey, California, and then I was sent to auto mechanics school, I guess because my testing showed that I had an aptitude for mechanical things, and I did enjoy the school.

In basic training, Grandma ("Mom") sent me cookies almost weekly, and each one would be wrapped in foil—there was never a broken one. Other guys got boxes of crumbs! I knew each of my cookies had been carefully wrapped with love.

For most of my life growing up, I had thought that I would only live until my early twenties, this was just a feeling I had, and I had pretty much just accepted that. At Thanksgiving time, a friend and I were going to fly to San Diego to be with our families for the holiday. It was a stormy evening when we finished classes and got to the airport in Monterey, only to find that all planes had been grounded because of the weather. We went back to the barracks thinking that we should just call home and let our folks know that we could not make it.

Then a car drove up outside the barracks and someone shouted, "Anyone want to go to San Diego?" Without even thinking, we both jumped in the backseat.

After several hours of driving, we went through the intersection where James Dean had been killed just three years earlier, and then we filled the gas tank in Bakersfield. It was cold and wet, and I was drowsy, and in those days, cars did not have seat belts, so as the car swerved and crashed into another car almost head-on, I went over the people in the front seat and through the windshield. The car went end over end, and I came back through the windshield. Coming back through saved me, for the car then landed on its roof and started rolling.

It seemed as though the car would never stop. Then everything went quiet, and I was going down a long tunnel with a light at the end. Everything was so peaceful, and then a voice coming from the light was saying, "I've changed my mind!" Then the wreckage continued, and the car slid on its top so long that my friend Jim's hair was singed through the top of the car!

The car was upside down, with all the gas pouring in on us, and my only thought was to get out. There was some light coming in through what had been a window, and I could see the door handle near my feet. I knew that if I pushed on the door it would open, but my left leg just didn't seem to be strong enough to move it. Then I tried my right leg and the door scraped open. I said, "Jim, we gotta get out—it's going to catch fire!" I pulled myself up on the door and got Jim out, not realizing how bad I looked, and then I tried to take a step but fell down in the mud.

A truck driver picked me up and put me in the front seat of his truck, where it was warm. My uniform was pretty much gone, and bones were almost sticking out of my left knee. My right hand was nearly crushed, my fingers shredded by the windshield, and my glasses had taken a lot of skin off my face.

The truck driver had also put Jim on the seat next to me, and as we sat there, I was more concerned about Jim; I thought he had brain damage because he just kept feeling his head and repeating things over and over. I realized later that he had just gone into shock at seeing me, not to mention because of the whole experience!

We sat looking at the wreckage of the two cars until ambulances arrived, and because they didn't want to change the position of my leg, they put me in the front seat of one of the ambulances. The ambulance was going about seventy when a hay truck pulled out in front of us. The ambulance spun out into a field, and I went into the dash, turning off a lot of switches. It took a while to get going again, but we finally arrived at the hospital.

As a nurse, Mother had always said that if you were in a strange place and needed medical attention, you should go to a Seventh-Day Adventist facility, as they had good training, and of all things, that was where I ended up.

As nurses gathered around cutting off the remains of my uniform and that proverbial "clean underwear" (I will guarantee you that after an accident like that, your underwear will not be clean!) and preparing me for surgery, I said, "I guess I should be blushing now?" All but one of the nurses said things along this line: "Oh we do this every day, and besides, we are all married." Then a little voice said, "I'm not!" After several days, I was moved to an army hospital, and I spent about two and a half months recovering.

I had essentially finished auto mechanics school, but when I got to my assignment at Fort Huachuca, they saw that one of my majors had been graphic arts, and they placed me, as the only military person, in a technical writing office.

I had to get to work early to mix chemicals for what was one of the earliest copy machines, which produced a muddy black copy with white letters. My job later would be to coordinate work between the technical writers, editors, a large art department, a photo lab, and the print plant. I learned early on that the print plant had a Xerox machine that was just supposed to be used for making paper plates for the new offset presses. I got to know the person who ran the Xerox machine, and even though regulations were strict about just using this machine for printing press plates, I could sometimes get him to make a copy on celluloid. This copy could then be used on the blue print machine in the art department to make as many sepia-toned copies as we needed.

It was several years after this that Xerox realized they had a gold mine in their technology for making copies, and we now take copy machines for granted. I think this was one of the best jobs I ever had, and I enjoyed working with such nice people.

My first confrontation with racial problems and hatred

My desk at the office faced Dee's, a heavyset black middle-aged woman, always smiling. Fort Huachuca is located about a hundred miles east of Tucson, Arizona, in the mountains, and I had only been there a short time when I got a letter from one of the chaperones from our church, who was with a work team that was in Tucson for Easter week.

When I got back to the office after lunch, I made the statement that I would like to go to Tucson to see the folks from home. Dee said, "I'm going into Tucson after work today to see my family, and you can ride with me."

I didn't know her at all, but she threw me the keys to her car as we left work, and I had driven about an hour when we came to the small town of Benson. I pulled the car over and stopped at one of the restaurants in town, saying, "I'll buy you dinner." She looked at me as if I should have known and said, "There's no place in town where I can eat." Having grown up in the San Diego area without black friends, this was something I knew nothing about.

That was the first time I had experienced anything like that, and it changed my thinking forever concerning how people are treated. Here was this lovely woman letting me drive her car, and we could not even go into a restaurant and eat together! Again, I think those are the good old days, without government regulation, that conservatives want to get back to. At that time, I did not realize that it was capitalism's need for cheap labor that had created slavery—and that was my first run-in with Jim Crow.

Chapter 9
Teaching

After discharge from the army and attending a graduate year in college, I got my first teaching job with the San Diego City Schools, teaching junior high. As a new teacher, I taught four subjects in four different classrooms and had lunch duty for two sessions. I hardly could remember where I should be next!

Good teachers make learning as interesting as possible when they realize that all students come to them with a different set of interests. Using these interests or introducing them to new subjects that may interest them will let the students learn easier, faster, and better. Learning by "doing" is the best way to educate. It has taken hundreds of years to create the problems we are experiencing in education, and there are no quick fixes. Critics of public education seem to have little knowledge of teaching and even less about learning. Most critics have a special agenda, and for the politicians, it is to get votes; for the religious zealot, it is to get money for religious schools; and these are just two examples of critics with their own agendas.

Critics are usually people who never taught in public schools, and oftentimes they never attended one. They usually attack teachers, and sometimes public schools in general, and they always want a quick fix.

Fifty years ago, when I first entered teaching, educators were trying to come up with a quick fix. At that time, it was team teaching, which helps because having two adults in a classroom lets one teacher teach while the other takes care of special needs, individual attention, and discipline. Discipline problems are frequently the result of emotional problems caused by a dysfunctional family, inherited psychological problems or chemical imbalances, or environmental chemicals.

You would think that after so many years of blaming teachers and schools, the critics, if they are truly interested in improving public schools, would quit their criticizing and make a serious effort to find out the true reasons children don't learn. I am afraid the subject just makes good fodder for politicians and those who have other agendas. I have also concluded that they do not want to know the truth, as it is my belief that learning problems have been caused by our capitalistic society over hundreds of years, and capitalists don't want the expense of cleaning up the mess they have caused.

It is counterproductive to take only high-performing students out of public schools, place them in private schools, and then compare the two. This does damage to teachers, to public schools, and to society in general.

It helps us understand learning problems if we review the teaching process, which is similar whether teaching English or auto mechanics. The material must first be organized into a logical learning order and then divided into understandable learning parts. The teacher then decides how to best present the information. The learning may take place by repetition, by doing a project such as a writing assignment, or by whatever method the teacher thinks might make the subject interesting and make the children want to learn. No matter what the subject, there must be an activity so that the learning is set to memory or learned by the students. A basic premise in teaching is that the teacher does not just present information; there should be stimulating action for learning to take place.

The second year of teaching, I was assigned to the school where I had done my student teaching, which was considered one of the roughest schools in the district. Because of some boundary line changes, the school had rapidly changed from predominantly white to predominantly black.

Getting ready to teach

I spent nights and weekends developing materials. I would take slides of examples of all the safety areas in the shop, and I made a recording of the safety test, with sample pictures of each item, and while recording, I would tap on a glass when it was time to change slides. I knew that most of the children had reading problems and could not pass the safety test, which they had to do if they were to work in the shop. In recording the safety test and playing it to them, they could all pass the test and work in the shop, which many past teachers did not think was a good idea. Having children out of their seats does create discipline problems, but I think it was for the best. One of my biggest problems was that many of the students would come back after school to work, and often they didn't want to go home.

One of the projects the students did was designing Christmas cards, each one cutting a linoleum block and writing a greeting for the inside, and we would print them on the letterpresses. When one of the boys quietly asked if he could do a Hanukkah card, I suddenly realized how naive I was. No students were the same, and I started enjoying all the differences even more.

One of the older metalworking teachers, who had started teaching at a neighboring school, told the story about the first time he let his students go from the classroom into the metal shop. He made the mistake of going in front of the students, only to turn around and see that one of the students had used a lighter to set fire to all his charts hanging on the wall.

My dad's cousin got a job in Los Angeles teaching metal shop, and the first time they used the forge, one of the students tossed a handful of .22 shells inside it. He left teaching for good. He said that it was as if someone had walked in with a gun and started shooting up the place, and once was enough for him.

Until you have had a fight in your classroom between two large girls, you don't know what teaching is all about. They start fighting over nothing and proceed to hair pulling and clothes ripping. When you try to break them up, they start in on you! Most of the time with boys, it seemed as though they really didn't want to fight, and if you could get between them, they would usually stop.

I sometimes had classes of thirty-four students that were classified "special and adjustments," and I'd had seven fights in one hour. A student might just say a quiet "oink" so that an overweight student could hear it, and a fight would start. One student's eyes shook, and someone would mimic him and shake his eyes, and a fight would start. Sometimes something as innocent sounding as "your mama" would start a fight.

In one of those classes, a student would sit and pull out one hair at a time and eat it. By the time he had pulled them all out, they would have started to grow in at the front, and he would start over again. I mentioned to the principal that I thought this student had a psychological problem that was affecting his learning, and the only thing the principal said was, "You aren't trained to make that diagnosis." This was almost fifty years ago, and while I knew I was not a trained psychologist, I don't think it takes a lot of training to know when a person has a serious problem that affects his learning.

How I learned about some of the things that affect student learning

Racism
I also taught art in that same room, which added some problems that I had to solve. A small black girl in one of these classes just glared at me and did little work, but because she was not a discipline problem, I did not take the time to contact her home.

Open house was early in the year, and the girl's grandmother attended. I began to explain the problem, and she listened attentively. Then she began to tell me the reason for her granddaughter living with her.

It was the early sixties, and this child had watched the KKK murder both her parents in the South. I was overwhelmed, as I had no idea that anything like that was taking place in the United States. Not being able to eat with Dee in a restaurant was one thing, but this was unbelievable to me. How was I, a white man—or anyone, for that matter—going to teach this girl after such a traumatic experience?

I also was in charge of producing the school annual, and we had an after-school staff consisting of all black students except for one boy. While we had letterpresses in the classroom, which most of the staff had learned how to work, the annual was being done using offset presses, which was still a rather new concept at that time. I had taught the annual staff the basics of how offset presses worked, and how pictures were prepared for printing. When it was time for our annual to be printed at a local printer, I scheduled a field trip for the staff to go see their annual being printed.

This was an interesting experience because it was obvious that the person from the print shop who was leading the tour was only talking to the Anglo student, and the black students noticed this at once. They just smiled and asked some of the most technical questions the guide had ever been asked, and they forced him to talk to them! The print shop had probably never had a black person tour before this group of very intelligent students.

1965, the Gompers Junior High School annual staff

Military discipline

One of my tall, thin black students was having a problem, so I sent a note home about the problem. I learned later that when the military father had seen the note, he had knocked his wife's front tooth out because she was supposed to be in control of such things.

Alcohol

The drunken mother of one of my small black students drove her car right up onto the front lawn of the school as school was getting out. She fell half out of the car with legs still inside. With most of the school watching and laughing, her son, my student, got her in the car, and his ninth-grade sister drove the car home. The next day I expressed to him how sorry I was at what had happened and he said, "Oh, we go every night at about two o'clock and get our mother from one of the local bars."

Private schools

Then there was that little black kid who was so disruptive, and was I glad when he transferred out of the class. However, he was back in a few days and when asked where he had been, he said that he had been sent to the local Catholic school. His explanation for returning to my class was that when the nun hit his hand with a ruler, he punched her in the belly, and that was why he was back with me.

The N-word

One day while I was teaching an art class in the graphic arts shop, the all-black class was cleaning up at the end of the hour, and the students began using the N word. I started giving it to them, letting them know that that word was never to be used. I had been reading the books of many black authors and had black friends now, so I was beginning to feel the hurt that that word embodies. The bell rang, ending the class, and as the children were leaving, one of the girls came up and took my hand and said, "It's okay, Mr. Doerr, you're as much a nigger as the rest of us!" This made me realize that when a black person uses it, the meaning can be quite different, for it may mean that one is strong enough to endure all that this word implies.

Even some of the best teachers can't handle bad situations

I could write an entire book about the experiences there, but let's just say that we usually lost many teachers, and the last year I was there, eighteen teachers just walked out the first week, not even returning for their coats.

They all got good jobs in other districts and were considered some of the best teachers when working with students that did not have the problems these children did.

Two adults in every classroom

Even the principal was run out—and was replaced by a new principal who at one time had been a teacher at this school and then a vice principal in another school. He provided every teacher in the school with a full-time aid. Two adults in every classroom allowed the teachers to teach and the students to get some of the attention they so desperately needed.

New experiences in the black world

During this time, I had decided to visit some friends back East at Christmastime, and a black friend was also going to be visiting family and friends in the East at that time; he asked if I would like to join him and meet some of his family and friends. I did, and this was a great learning experience for me. He was quite dark, but his mother was near white. In some places, we would stay in the white section of town, and in others the black section, and I met a lot of wonderful people. I probably would not have been able to have an experience like that if it had not been for him.

One late evening in Cleveland, when we were staying with his brother in the black part of town, we stopped at a doughnut shop to get something for breakfast. I jumped out of the car and ran into the store, with overcoat and hat on, looking like a vice officer or gangster, and the poor black kid behind the counter threw up his hands, probably thinking he was being robbed, as that would be the only reason for a white man to be in that neighborhood at that time of night—or anytime, for that matter.

That year at school was much better, but I got sick and was told I had leukemia. Looking back, I think that I had just not been used to the extreme cold back East and had gotten run down. I was so sick that I didn't think I could go on teaching, and I handed in my resignation, effective at the end of the school year, which was not far off. More tests revealed that I just had a bad case of mononucleosis, but I decided that I would finish my master's degree while substitute teaching the next year, and then I would try a new career.

I started working on my master's, trying different topics, only to realize what I had known most of my life, and that is that *education and learning are work, and the only way to accomplish education goals is to study subject matter that you are interested in. I had always been interested in pipe organs, and I was able to work this subject into a master's project.*

After I finished what seemed like a never-ending job and submitted all the copies to the graduate office, they called me in. Thinking the worst, that all my work had been rejected, I was surprised when the man sitting on the other side of the desk said that most of the work they received was just downright boring; mine was the most interesting they had received in a long time!

I had used information and pictures from an organ rebuilding job that I had worked on the summer of my thirtieth birthday. Incidentally, a few years ago, on my seventieth birthday, we were tuning that organ, and the fellow back in the chambers came out with a newspaper that had been laminated and put in the chambers about the organ rebuilding forty years before. He read the article aloud, and it named all of us that had done the work all those years ago. I had worked on that organ on my thirtieth birthday, and there I was on my seventieth!

World's fair in Montreal, Canada, 1967

Toward the end of the summer of 1967, I decided to travel to some of the eastern cities, and I stopped to see Uncle Bob and Aunt Monica, who were in Boston while he was a batting coach for the Red Sox. That was exciting, as they were in the playoffs for the World Series, and the whole town was crazy about baseball. I then took the bus to Montreal, Canada, for the world's fair.

During this time, racial tensions were building, and while on the bus, I was sitting behind two women, one from Canada and one from the United States. I wasn't paying much attention to what they were talking about—until I heard the woman from Canada say, "You were lucky you got first choice and got the American Negro; we had to take the French!" I almost dove under the seat, thinking there would be a riot at any moment.

I subbed almost every day the next year, and I took night classes. There were about three months left in the school year when I was offered a long-term substitute job in the Sweetwater District, south of San Diego, near the Mexican border. I let them know that I would do it, but I was interested in leaving teaching, so three months would be it.

Teaching auto theory in Spanish

I was teaching auto mechanics theory, and no one told me that many of the students did not speak English, only Spanish! I immediately realized that I would have to enlist the help of one good student in each class who was bilingual, and he would be guaranteed a good grade for his help. He would read in Spanish to the non-English-speaking students and help them understand and take the tests and pass the course so that they could go on and take the auto shop class the next year. This worked out well and solved a problem that would have resulted in a discipline nightmare and many failed students.

My first racial incident where I was attacked

I was involved in a racial incident when walking with a black friend one evening. I heard the words "nigger lover," and the next thing I knew, I was going up in the air and coming down in the gutter between two parked cars. My shoulder was broken in two places, with bones displaced, broken ribs, and facial cuts. This sort of thing was not uncommon in those days, as there was still segregation and Jim Crow in effect in the South. Even out here in the West, white people who associated with black people were considered the enemy. This experience was mostly a physical one for me, but for composer George Gershwin, it was psychological pain.

He was essentially thought of as a nigger lover because he wrote the beautiful music to what is now considered one of the most important American operas of the twentieth century, *Porgy and Bess*, about African Americans. He died at thirty-eight years old, being told that *Porgy and Bess* would be a failure because the general public would not be interested in an opera about Negroes. His music should make all of us proud and raise our national esteem.

I was only two weeks into auto theory teaching when the principal asked if I would teach driving for the summer. I knew that teaching teenagers to drive was one of the easier jobs, and I could use the money, so I took it. Another two weeks passed, and the principal asked me to teach art the following year, as that teacher was leaving. He said that I would have my own room all to myself, no sharing, making it hard for me to refuse. While the students there had many problems, many speaking only Spanish, and a large population coming from military families, there generally were not the discipline problems I had encountered at my previous assignments. Many of the kids went surfing at the beach down the street before coming to class.

My first time teaching one subject in one classroom

I taught art that next year and actually was able to enjoy work, but it was work! I remember leaving the house at six o'clock one Friday morning, teaching all day, grading art projects, running to get some dinner, and then chaperoning the football game and the dance afterward. I got back home about one in the morning!

At the beginning of one class hour, I had just started to take the roll, and I looked up to see one of the students with his eyes closed and his head on his desk. Someone said that he had taken a handful of pills on the way to class. The only thing I could think of to do was scoop him up and run with him to the school nurse. Thankfully, he was small. I laid him across some chairs as the nurse exclaimed, "What's wrong with him?" I told her that the kids just said that he had taken a handful of pills.

Suicide

In art classes, a lot of time is spent helping students with their ideas, and I would go from student to student. One day I was next to two girls who were talking about a sailor who had set himself on fire atop a mountain across the border. I told them about my pyrophobia and said that if I had witnessed something like that, it could possibly cause me permanent psychological damage. I related a story about our neighbor who had just put a garden hose up the exhaust pipe of her car, with the engine running, and climbed in the backseat with the other end under her coat that was over her head. No pain, not like burning to death, and not as upsetting to onlookers.

I heard from someone the next year that one of these girls had gone to New England for the summer and then disappeared. In the fall, when the leaves began to fall off one of the big trees, there she was, high in the branches, hanging with her teddy bear in one arm and her guitar in the other. Suicide is a growing problem among our children—and just one of the symptoms of a much bigger problem.

1968 My first trip to the Caribbean

I stayed a few days in Jamaica and then arrived in Haiti after dark, when the electricity was off, which occurred regularly, and I was the only white person getting off the plane; they didn't have many tourists in those days. I found out that part of the reason was because of the movie *The Comedians*. I stayed in the Plaza hotel, across from the palace, and the only other guest was a young Jamaican college student who was accused of trying to start a revolution and was confined to the hotel. This is also where I learned that those big green lizards that hang around the light bulbs in your room are really your friends, as they eat large quantities of those stinging insects! You don't just visit Haiti; you experience it!

This is where I first learned about the young kids who offer to be tour guides. They truly are a great deal of help, especially if you buy something. They will find a box and carry your things while helping you find the post office. In third world countries, these kids are happy getting pocket change, and if you want, you have a friend for life.

I next visited the US Virgin Islands. Martin Luther King Jr. and Robert Kennedy had just been assassinated, and I was the only white person on a small ferry going from St. Thomas at Red Hook Landing, on the Fourth of July, to St. John. When I reached St. John, they searched me for weapons before I could get off the boat, as they didn't want a white man from the mainland coming and spoiling their celebration. I heard steel drums and ate goat stew for the first time; I did not feel uncomfortable being about the only white person there.

Another day, I took a seaplane over to St. Croix and bounced across the island with the locals in a taxi, sharing food and having a good time. There was a problem trying to get back on the seaplane to get back to St. Thomas, for a storm had come up, and everyone got on the floating pier at once. It started to sink, and then people got on the plane so fast that it started to tip over, causing water to come in the door. Finally, all had boarded, and we took off. Everything was fine until we started to descend for the landing. All of a sudden, the pilot gunned the engine, and we climbed rapidly up and over a small sailboat that had come out from a small cove without warning. We just missed the mast!

When I was ready to leave the Virgin Islands, I got to the airport quite early, only to find that my plane was taxiing to take off. The ticket agent said, "Oh, don't worry. I'll stop them." She did, and the plane came back.

When I boarded, I asked the little black flight attendant if the plane stopped before getting to Barbados. She just laughed and kept repeating, "Do we stop before we get to Barbados?" Well, we stopped on about ten small islands, landing on what seemed like the sides of volcanoes, beaches, banana fields, and in cane fields. And all the flight attendant said when we got to Barbados and we were getting off was, "Did we stop before we got here?"

Later I learned that not only did LIAT stand for Leeward Island Air Transport, but the locals usually said that it stood for "leaves island at any time" or "look into alternate transportation," which probably didn't exist or would be hard to find. I have gone together with others going to an island and chartered a small plane for no more than a ticket on the scheduled airline. I could probably write a separate book about my summer travels in the Caribbean, with lots of interesting adventures and meeting many wonderful travelers and local people.

I made friends in Barbados and returned almost every summer to stay at guesthouses that cost only four dollars a day with meals—not on the beach but within walking distance. These were on all the islands and were frequently where the locals from other islands stayed. Barbados had just gotten its independence from England, so politics was an interesting subject.

Over the years, I spent time on twenty-one islands in the Caribbean, and I found that not only does each island have different rum, a by-product of sugar making, but each one has a different culture all its own. Slavery and the destruction of the family seem to have produced a different outcome on each island.

Barbados is respected for its education system and strong families, and the little island of Dominica seems to have little family structure. I talked to a fellow once who was in charge of shipments by sea, and he said that it was almost impossible to take shipments to Dominica because of disorganization and pilferage. I hope things have improved in the many years since then.

Chapter 10
Trying to Leave Teaching

After returning from the Caribbean in 1968, I went to work as a probation officer at juvenile hall, only to find while checking rooms my first night of work that out of the population of twenty-nine in that unit, ten had been former students of mine!

There was the small boy whose mother had driven her car up on the school lawn as school was getting out, the tall kid whose mother's tooth had been knocked out by his military father, and the one who had been sent to Catholic school, only to return. There were seven others, most of whom had never given me any trouble while teaching, and I had no idea why they were being detained.

Sometime later, in another unit, there was the fellow that I had carried to the nurse's office from the high school art class. One day they called down from the control desk, saying they were sending a new kid down, which they would do if the detainee was not a problem, and we would just watch him come down the hall.

As this boy approached me, tears started rolling down his cheeks, and he said, "Oh, what are you doing here Mr. Doerr?" He handed me his information card, which I gave to the lead person, and he looked at it and said, "Put him in the first isolation room." I did so, and when I returned to the control area where the room assignment board was, there was a red circle around his name, for all to see that he was homosexual. His military stepfather had the police bring him here when he found out he was gay. He later was committed to the nearby mental hospital.

One day I came to work and was assigned to the intake unit, where there was an unruly black kid in an isolation room. We could not process him in until he settled down. I asked him several times if he would like some dinner, and he just gave me a lot of foul language. Finally, I told him that I was not going to open the door until he settled down, as he might hurt me, and he laughed! He looked at me and said, "I'm okay now. Could I have something to eat?" I went to the kitchen and got a tray of food. Opening the door, I set it on the shelf, and he actually thanked me. After he finished, I opened the door and asked if he was ready to get dressed in (turn in his outside cloths for juvenile hall clothes), and he asked if he couldn't have more to eat, so I went and got more and said that he could eat it outside of the cell, next to the desk where I would be.

He started telling me about how the police had come to school at lunchtime and put handcuffs on him while all the kids watched and laughed. He admitted that he had done something wrong, but he said they knew where he lived and could have come to his house at any time. I told him about teaching at his school and said that I had a good experience teaching wood shop there in summer school. I was talking to him like another human being, something I don't think he had happen very often. Suddenly, he jumped up, threw his arms around me, and started crying.

The people at the main desk saw this and were not happy about it, as of course, we should not have that kind of contact with the detainees, but it had happened so fast that I did not see it coming. I saw him later after he had been assigned to a unit, and he would always smile. I wondered if this fellow had ever had anyone treat him like a person.

Greg Louganis

During my time at juvenile hall, I worked in various units, and several times I worked in the unit that housed the youngest detainees. I didn't know it at the time, but one of these youngsters was the future world-famous Olympic diver Greg Louganis, who would win gold medals for the United States diving team.

About a year and a half after leaving juvenile hall, when I was walking across the school campus at Grossmont High School, a young kid ran up to me and said, "Hi, coach." I looked at him and said that the only one who would call me "coach" would be someone who had been at juvenile hall. He said that he had been, and that I had worked in his unit. I asked what he was doing at Grossmont High School, and he said that he was taking part in a gymnastics competition on campus. I asked his name, and he said Greg Louganis.

Greg was an adopted child whose birth parents were only fifteen years old when he was born, and one parent was Samoan, so he had dark skin, and I later learned from reading Greg's book *Breaking the Surface* that growing up he had been called "nigger," the most hurtful word ever invented. Just being adopted carries a lot of baggage with it, and I am sure it contributed to some of his life problems, but it seems as though he has come to grips with these problems and is doing well now.

The word nigger was invented during slavery and Jim Crow, and it embodies an enormous amount of hurt and degradation. Perhaps Greg achieved what he did to prove to the world that he was strong enough, intelligent enough, and talented enough to overcome everything that that word implies.

As a "coach" at juvenile hall one had to play football almost every day with the detainees, and I didn't think this was what I wanted to spend the rest of my life doing, so when a job opened up near San Jose, California, in the Santa Clara juvenile court schools, I applied, interviewed, and got it.

Chapter 11
James Boys Ranch

They had eight to ten students who could not function in any of their classes, and they needed someone to do what they could for them. I thought that I could easily handle that many students.

James Boys Ranch, a facility for high school boys, was located near Morgan Hill, California, where a steep mountain formed the east border, and a river curved around the south, west, and north sides so no fences were needed. The only access was via a bridge over the small river. On the same land, but much farther to the south, was a facility for junior high boys.

There had been heavy rains in the days before I was to report, and I drove up in my 1966 Mustang, only to find that the river had washed out the land on both sides of the bridge and there were some makeshift planks on each side that would allow one to walk across, over the swirling waters below, which I did. Waiting was a station wagon driven by a tall black teenager, whom I soon learned was one of the detainees that had worked his way up to that responsible position.

Sometime later, after he had been released, we would be standing next to each other at a standing-room only lecture at San Jose State College, being given by Alex Haley, who was telling about his research on the book he was writing, which would be called *Roots*.

As I look back on my experiences at James Boys Ranch, I know that it was one of the most educational experiences I'd ever had. The people who organized the probation part knew what they were doing, and the persons who organized the school part were also exceptional. There were essentially three programs and facilities; the one where I would be working was for high school boys, and part of their responsibility was to raise the meat for all three facilities. Quite a distance down the road, the junior high boys would raise the vegetables. All the boys were learning how to be responsible for their own survival. Across the valley was the girls' facility, where each girl had a horse that she had to be completely responsible for.

The organization of the probation part was interesting. Boys would enter as "D" boys, having no privileges or freedoms, and would have to work their way up to "A" boys, at which time they could drive the vehicles, trucks, and cars while working on the ranch. If they messed up, they would have to start over again, and if they tried to leave or "escape," they knew that they would go to the California Youth Authority, which would not be good.

The schools were organized by subject matter, but every teacher had sets of textbooks at reading levels from first grade to twelfth, and they all had graded word lists that would be handed to entering students—and they did come and go frequently. Each student would read a graded word list until he stopped, and a number above the word indicated their reading level. He would then be assigned a book at that level. The teachers would lecture and have projects, just like most classrooms, but the students could do the work in the textbooks at their own level and speed.

There were fifteen-minute breaks during each hour, and all teachers were expected to work with the students at this time. The teachers taught them to ride unicycles, jump on a trampoline, and do many other things that offered positive interaction between teenager and adult, something that most of these kids had seldom had.

The originator of this school was a talented Mr. Smith, who was an accomplished musician, and he had recognized that one boy had musical talents. He taught him to play on the piano twenty-eight pieces of popular music using the chord method. All the students appeared to be succeeding to their fullest, except for the ones that were in my charge, and the administration just said to do whatever I could with them.

I knew that they would all have reading problems, so I gathered a lot of different books that I thought they might be interested in, as I knew from my own experience that Dick and Jane would be counterproductive. I look back now and realize that all of my eight or ten students had what we now recognize as ADD or ADHD; we just did not know anything about it then.

With few students and this system of graded textbooks and reading level lists, I could work with individuals while the rest worked from different textbooks. Working with each student on his reading individually worked well with most of the students, but one bright Mexican boy stands out. He was a true dyslexic, and educators did not know much about dyslexia in those days.

In retrospect, I realized that a dyslexic's education should take place almost as though he were blind; and we should demand that textbook publishers provide audio recordings for the blind and dyslexic so they can learn the subject matter without having to read.

This one boy could sound out words, knowing all the sounds each letter represented, but his brain just did not process the sounds into words. He would try and try, and even cry, and he would say, "Mr. Doerr, I want to read," but that just did not happen. I asked him to stop and think what he would like to do for his life's work, and after some thinking, he said that he would like to be a barber. I looked at him and said, "You don't have to read to be a barber." I think his whole life changed at that moment, and if I remember correctly, I looked into barber schools and got information for him. A large percentage of people in prisons have reading problems and ADD and ADHD.

At the end of the semester, I was called into the office and told that all the students had been given achievement tests, and that many of my students had improved their reading levels approximately two years for every month I had them.

During that summer, I came home and was offered a job at the high school I had graduated from. I would have a full-time position as the work experience coordinator, too good of a job to turn down, and I would be back home with family and many friends.

Chapter 12

Teaching at Grossmont High School

The first year I was there, several of the counselors and I converted a classroom into a career center with two offices, one for me and one for the counselor that specialized in vocational training. For the next twenty-five years, I would have the little office isolated in back. We had just gotten this facility set up when students began to come in, realizing it was a nice place to hang out when they had a few free moments. Once when I was back in my little office and several girls were sitting out in the center with no other adult, and not knowing I could overhear their conversation, they were telling each other about the first time they had sex. One girl spoke up and said that the first time for her was when she was raped, and the girls all gasped and said, "Oh no." And she said, "Oh, that's okay; he was so small that I was still a virgin afterward!" I went over backward in my chair, and the girls heard the crash and ran out!

Another work experience program that was developed while I worked at Grossmont High was having the students design a house, draft the plans, order the materials, and actually build the house, which was then auctioned off. I think this program practically paid for its self. One of the former principals still lives in one of these homes.

Another one of the programs we developed was the Exploratory Work Experience Program, where students could go out and observe and work, nonpaid, in a large number of professions. Students could work and observe in the real world, making them begin to feel a part of it.

This was helpful for those who were not finding academic success at school. The program offered them the opportunity to explore a subject before spending a lot of money training for something they might not really care for. Moreover, employers could get to know their future employees, and many students were hired because they had worked in the program.

Why do we insist on keeping children in failing situations when some have had a lifetime of failing? It's important to find something else where they can be productive citizens rather than turning to negative gangs.

**Pop and Mom on their last anniversary together.
He would die the following January.**

I had bought two lots near downtown San Diego, and my grandfather told me never to sell them because they could be developed into one property and made more desirable. I did not heed his advice, thinking that because I could double my money in keeping them for just two years, I was doing well. I had bought the two for three thousand dollars, and I sold them for six thousand dollars. This seemed like a lot of money then, but I had sold the lots with house plans, which the new owners used, and the property sold for about $1.5 million a few years ago. Always listen to your elders!

One of my former teachers that I was now teaching with told me to use the money I had made from the property and take an around-the-world tour that some of her friends had taken the year before. She gave me a brochure, and I sent in a deposit. I think it was one of those life-changing events, as you will see from my description of the trip.

The trip was sponsored by the California Teachers Association and organized by British Airways. It only cost $1,995 dollars for airfare, hotels, most meals, and most everything else.

Chapter 13
Around the World

I went a week early and planned to meet the rest of the group in Hawaii, where I had friends. The highlight there was going out to Pearl Harbor and to the WWII memorial. Standing above the USS *Arizona*, with bubbles still percolating up from where over a thousand servicemen are entombed, I couldn't help but remember December 7, 1941.

I met the group, which was mostly teachers, with the exception of three Catholic priests, and we went to the airport for the flight to Tokyo. Japan is a contrast of old and new, consisting of seeing beautiful old buildings, shrines, and temples and then riding on high-speed trains. It was all a thrill for me.

The world's fair in Osaka was excellent, and it was fun comparing it to the one I had attended in Montreal a few years before. We saw many beautiful sights in Japan and even spent a night in the mountains overlooking a lake. We saw country people and women carrying their babies on their backs. Our next stop was Hong Kong.

The first day in Hong Kong, almost everyone was fitted for clothing so that they would be completed when we got ready to leave. The tour included a great deal of sightseeing in each place, and in the spare time, I rode the ferryboats, double-deck trolleys, and the cable car up the mountain, where the views of the city were spectacular.

1970, around-the-world tour group

After a few days in Hong Kong, we were off to the fairyland of the Orient, Bangkok, with its Grand Palace and other beautiful buildings, including the Wat Phra Keo (housing the beautiful Emerald Buddha). There were boat trips on the *klongs* (canals), passing by the colorful floating markets and boathouses with picturesque scenes of canal life. Then it was time to head for an even more exotic place, Kathmandu, Nepal.

As we were landing in Calcutta, India, to refuel, I could see a trolley pole touching the high voltage wire of a streetcar. It had people all over the top and sides and was pushing people out of the way as it went down the street! If ever a place needed birth control, it is Calcutta.

Then we were on to Kathmandu, Nepal, where the plane circled around until the pilot found a hole in the clouds to dive through. Suddenly, we were in another exotic land with mountains on all sides that were sculpted with curves to form land flattened for crops, probably rice. This made the mountains seem as though they had been decorated with giant lace. There were large temples with square towers with great eyes painted on them, as though to watch over the valley. As soon as the cows were chased off the runway, our plane landed.

We were up early the next morning for the drive to see the sun rising on Mount Everest—I didn't think that I would ever have an experience like that—and then back to the interesting city of Kathmandu for sightseeing.

There always seemed to be a crowd of people looking up at an old two-story building, and then I realized why. Carved into each of the roof supports around the eaves were figures in every imaginable sexual position. This, I guess, was sex education illustrated as a useful art and decoration!

As we traveled around the world, I noticed that men frequently held hands when walking together. I asked some of the locals who were helping me buy some drums about this, and they assured me that it did not have the same meaning as it did in the United States; it was just a sign of heterosexual friendship.

Our group got to go into some of the temples with the big eyes, and there were many prayer wheels. Written prayers were placed inside, and every time a priest went by, they would turn the wheel. There were also small ones made of copper. Each one had a handle and a chain with a weight attached so that it could be held and spun around with the prayer inside. I bought one of these, and the following year, I was asked to speak to a second-grade class. The topic was children around the world. I took along an entire box of different containers, handmade musical instruments, and many other things, including the prayer wheel.

The children were all attentive and interested, and I later received many notes of appreciation, including one I will never forget, for the child wrote, *Mr. Doerr, your talk was very good, but you forgot one thing. You didn't tell us how the prayers got to heaven!*

From Kathmandu, we flew to Banaras. The next morning, we were out on the Ganges, where people were bathing, while a distance away, there were burning ghats, with human ashes being poured into the river.

Leaving Banaras and arriving in Agra, I was suddenly aware of the extremes in India. As I viewed the Taj Mahal, I was stunned at how much more beautiful the building is than its pictures portray. We returned that evening to see it by the light of a full moon; yes, the tour was planned that way. It truly is like a giant piece of jewelry set with precious stones.

Then we were on to Jaipur, with its vast gardens, exquisite Maharaja's City Palace, the eighteenth-century astronomical observatory, and the elaborate Palace of the Winds. There were women in wide shirts, and men in bright turbans, and this is where camel caravans come in from the desert.

We visited New Delhi and saw the Red Fort before driving through Chandni Chowk, Delhi's busy and colorful bazaar. Our next stop was back up in the mountains to Srinagar, Kashmir, where we stayed in beautiful all-natural wood houseboats on Lake Dahl. While I enjoyed going into town in the two-wheeled horse-drawn carts, I was most interested in the workings of the houseboat.

I would awaken early in the morning and hear the houseboy and cook pumping water out of the lake to a tank on the roof of the boat, but I would also hear the water from flushing toilets going into the lake! Worst of all, most everyone insisted on drinking bottled water and toward the end of our stay I noticed that the houseboy, having no knowledge of sanitation, would fill the bottles out of the lake and put them in the refrigerator! Unfortunately I did not notice these things until it was too late and the others had already drunk the water. By the time we got to Africa, we had many sick people. I carried tablets that purified the drinking water I used, so I did not get sick.

We went back to New Delhi and then to Bombay for a short afternoon and dinner at the Taj Mahal Hotel, and then we were back to the airport for the flight to Nairobi, Africa, where, going through customs and immigration, several of our group were put in quarantine because they had not gotten their cholera shots. In one section of Kathmandu we had visited, we learned that five people had died with cholera the day we were there. The people without shots would miss part of the safari.

My first morning in Nairobi, I was walking down the street, near the Hilton, looking at a Masai girl with all her beautiful beaded collars, and I almost ran into Elizabeth Taylor. She was wearing the most expensive coat in the world at that time, and the two extremes were fascinating, to say the least.

As we were leaving Nairobi the next morning starting our safari, there were ostriches running alongside our van. We arrived at Kilaguni Lodge in time for lunch, which was interesting since the lodge is constructed of local stone with thatched roofs and open areas, and beautiful wild birds would fly in and sit on the back of our chairs while we were eating.

Most of the views were directed at several watering holes, where about every animal imaginable would come, in kind of a pecking order, and each group seemed to know when it was their turn. Our sleeping rooms also had views, and there were lights on the watering holes so that you could watch at any time of the night.

Near Kiaguni Lodge is Mzema Springs, with an underwater viewing station where you can see hippos under the water. If I were to return to East Africa, I think I would just go to Kilaguni Lodge and stay a week or two, letting the animals come to me!

After a couple of nights there, we went on to Arusha in Tanzania, seeing the sun set on Mount Kilimanjaro; I never thought I would get to see the sun rise on Mount Everest and then a few days later set on Mount Kilimanjaro!

One early morning in Arusha, I went out for a walk not far from town, but still kind of in the wild, and I was enjoying the beautiful Poinciana trees with their spectacular red-orange blossoms when I realized that two teenaged Masai boys had come up and were watching me. One came over and picked up one of the large seedpods that had fallen from one of the trees and opened it, taking out the seeds. He took my hand, placed the seeds in it, and said, "Take these home and plant them, and you will have some beautiful trees like ours."

The next summer, I would go to college in West Africa and meet a Masai student working on his master's. He would tell me how bad it was to be circumcised at about eighteen years old while the entire village looked on. One could not show any sign of pain, even though it may have been a dull instrument inflicting the pain. He didn't think he would have his sons endure this ritual. He could not wait to get home to his normal diet, for he had not gotten used to the vegetables and meat served in the school cafeteria. Another thing I learned from him is that people we consider primitive are usually well ahead of us in teaching their children how to be adults and parents.

We tend to think of the Masai as being rather uncivilized because they take the blood from their cattle and mix it with milk for food, without harming the animal. They think we are uncivilized and not logical because we kill our animals and eat the meat.

We were on safari for about eight days, going to many animal reserves and to Ngorongoro Crater, and I enjoyed meeting lots of new and different people. One of the most interesting was our driver for that week, whom I got to know while talking to him in the evenings.

He asked me not to tell the others on the trip, as they might not understand, but he had been active in the group that had fought for independence trying to overthrow the British in order to end colonialism, and he had actually killed many white people. The Europeans killed off the indigenous people while taking over the United States, but in Africa, most of the colonists were defeated. The outside world makes enormous amounts of goods from African products such as timber, fruits, nuts, chocolate, diamonds, gold, and many other minerals, while leaving the Africans poor.

The tour continued on to Addis Ababa, Ethiopia, were I could not resist buying large amounts of local handicrafts, which all of Africa has in abundance. I actually bought more than would fit in my suitcase, and I would later ship many boxes home.

Because I had grown up in a baseball family, I had been around many famous people, but I had never asked for an autograph. Sidney Poitier was staying in the same hotel as us, and one night at dinner, he and his daughter were dancing. He grew tired and sat down next to me at our table. We talked for a while, and I told him how my students at James Boys Ranch had enjoyed my reading his book to them. I then asked for his autograph, and I remembered how Aunt Monica had said that it is when they don't ask for autographs that you should worry. He smiled and signed it: "Happiness always, Sidney Poitier."

Next was Egypt, with the fascinating Egyptian Museum, pyramids, and sphinx, and then we went up the Nile to Luxor, with all the beautiful ancient temples, and then across the river to the Valley of the Kings. We passed Hatshepsut's temple, and then I experienced one of the highlights of my life: entering Tutankhamen's tomb. Later in the day, I spent hours wandering through the temples of Karnack before our flight back to Cairo.

After some time in Cairo, we were on to Athens, Greece, and all the many museums and the dream of a lifetime, the climb up the Propylaea at the Acropolis to see the Erechtheum and the Parthenon.

Then there was London, with all the museums, plays, and the wonderful public transportation systems, with double-deck buses and underground trains.

I finished this trip in New York with friends, sharing not only my travel memories but many of the things that I had gathered along the way. When I was in an African marketplace, I bargained for a whole bunch of items, such as beautiful hand-carved teak combs. I would get a bargain, and my friends would get useful gifts.

Chapter 14
College in West Africa

T he next year, I found out about an educational trip to West Africa for the summer, and it offered six college credits. We, as students, would stay in dormitories with the African students at four different colleges and universities in four different countries in West Africa.

We all met at the airport in Los Angeles for the flight to Paris, where we stayed in a college dorm outside the city and had a whole day to explore Paris, the Louvre, the Eifel Tower, and many of the other things I had always wanted to see in that beautiful city.

Study tour group, West Africa

Sierra Leone

Getting off the plane in Sierra Leone, I was immediately aware that this was not a normal tourist attraction. Fourah Bay College, the oldest college in West Africa could not have been a better place to start this educational journey. This was where African college students were brought from all over the continent to train people from Canada and the United States to be Peace Corps volunteers. When we arrived, there were no Peace Corps people to be trained, so we had the African students all to ourselves, and we talked well into the night about life in their villages, their traditions, and their living conditions and religions, getting to know some wonderful people.

We had African professors who lectured on African culture and history as well as local issues, and I felt rather uneducated, even with seven years of college and a master's degree. I'd known so little about this continent and its people, culture, and history.

Dugout canoe, West Africa

The day after we arrived, we were down by the ocean, and some teenage boys took me out in a dugout canoe just like American Indians made. I would later realize that the beaches of the west coast of Africa are frequently lined with these boats and occasionally an abandoned building where slaves were kept, waiting for the ships to take them on that dreaded voyage.

We all noticed right away that there was unusually good bread served in the school cafeteria, where some of the food was a little hard to get used to, and I decided to find out where it was coming from. After questioning several sources, I found the large beehive-type ovens, identical to those used by American Indians. Immigrants from a neighboring country were making the bread. It was just a few days later that the wonderful bread stopped being served, and we learned that the bakers had been deported.

Beehive oven, Sierra Leone

After morning lectures, there were short field trips in the afternoons, but some days we got up early in the morning for special longer trips. One of these was to a diamond-mining town, where a good road had just been completed, and we were told that the younger people there might never have seen white people.

Sure enough, when I was walking down the street in the tropical heat, a small child appeared between two buildings, took one look at me, and went into hysteria. His father came running from behind one of the buildings, and scooping the child up, he looked at me and said, "Oh! Big red man!" At lunch, we had many children staring through windows at us, and I'm sure we must have looked like people from another planet ... or maybe people returned from the dead.

Everyone was proud of the new hydroelectric dam that the United States had helped build, and we were taken to see it. The people in charge told us about it—and how much it meant to them. There is high rainfall there, so hydroelectric is certainly the appropriate and the cheapest way to provide power and water for the city. And it is far better for a foreign country to provide something like a dam rather than give money to a government that might help keep it in power when the people might like to get rid of it.

Boys from Lake Village

There was another early morning trip to the interior, where there was a crater lake with a very poor village along its shores. We were met at the top of the crater by four teenage boys who were excited to see visitors; we always had someone along who knew tribal traditions and the proper way to enter a village. As we made our way down the trail to the village, the older boy wanted to discuss with me who was going to be the Democratic vice president in the next election in the United States! These children were so poor that they did not have clothing, just cloth roped around them, but there was at least one transistor radio in the village, and the entertainment in the evenings was to listen to international news and discuss it among the elders.

They only got mail once a week and had to walk four miles for that, but the young man escorting me to his village had a magazine on space travel, which I felt quite inadequate discussing with him. Just because these teenagers were poor certainly did not mean that they were not intelligent, and I soon learned that most Africans speak at least six different languages, and usually one of them is English. I couldn't help but think how exciting it would be to have these children in a classroom; they would devour every educational thing presented to them. Moreover, the respect they had for elders and educators made me feel quite inadequate and perhaps undeserving.

Polygamy

We went to a village and met three wives of one of the men in the tribe, and this was my first encounter with polygamy, which is still common in Africa. It seems to have worked for them for many thousands of years. The first wife usually approves of any future wives and frequently welcomes more hands to do all the work that is required to survive in the independent social organization. Each wife has duties to perform, and they do each others' hair and take care of each others' children, even nursing them when necessary.

Our African professors frequently told us that one of the reasons Africans accept the Muslim religion a little easier than Christianity is because Africa is basically polygamous.

Wife #1 spinning, just like American Indians

Wife #2 using mortar and pestle; American Indians frequently used stone grinding tools

Wife #3 weaving mats

African women squat down to give birth, letting gravity do some of the work. The newborn child immediately goes on the mother's back, and the mother senses all the child's needs, avoiding trauma to the child. The only time I have heard an African baby or young child cry was that day when the little one came from between the buildings and saw me, and then his father was immediately there to comfort him. Babies are bathed in love and for the first few years only leave their parents' touch when they choose.

In his book *The Primal Scream*, Dr. Arthur Janov mentions that primitive peoples raise their children to be non-neurotic people who are not compulsive and not supportive of a capitalistic society. They don't have emotional pain caused by traumatic experiences as children, so they don't have the need to self-medicate, compulsively eat—or do anything compulsively, for that matter—or escape from emotional pain by buying things. In some tribes, the only things that some might consider "theirs" are the pots they cook with, and they are ceremoniously broken at their funeral services!

Children receiving unconditional love and no trauma

American Indian cultures were almost identical to Africans in their religious practices, raising children, growing crops, and even in their weaving, pottery, and basketry. In the United States, Indians readily took in escaped slaves because of all the cultural likenesses, and Indians usually had respect for darker skin and its ability to withstand the sun's rays.

Bunce Island

The next experience was one of the most emotional of all. We took a barge over to Bunce Island, where slaves had been stored and where few seldom go now, and there we saw the big stone buildings that are evidence of that dreadful time in history. Vines cover them now, but the buildings and dungeons where slaves had waited for the unknown almost seemed haunted with all those souls that had been taken from loving families to await their uncertain futures.

This was where that first link in the neurotic chain began, starting when they were torn from their loving families, and the voyage to come would be just the start of a short life of broken families, abuse, and misery.

Our group entering the slave-holding dungeons on Bunce Island, Sierra Leone

I am writing this on the Fourth of July, and I looked at the study guide that our African professors had prepared, and we were on Bunce Island on the Fourth of July in 1971. This was our independence day, but it was the end of independence for the people who had been imprisoned there. I don't think it was by accident that the professors planned the trip for that day.

Walking on the sands and picking up beads that had been torn from people's wrists and ankles before the shackles were put on was extremely emotional, but nothing like descending into the caverns where the enslaved had been stored. Approximately nine black teachers literally held each other and cried, and all of us had tears running down our cheeks.

This was one of the places where the capitalistic need for cheap labor started the psychological destruction that is passed on from generation to generation, and that teachers today have to try to overcome. Sometimes the emotional pain causes people to excel, but more often, it is educationally debilitating and generally self-destructive. This was one of the places where the first link in the neurotic chain was forged, and each generation adds a new link. It is interesting to note that sugar is frequently considered a love substitute, and

among the things that slaves would be producing was sugar, the love substitute
for neurotics!

Going to school in West Africa made me realize that socialism worked well
there for thousands of years, and there is a difference between socialism and
communism. and dictator and elected leaders.

Ivory Coast

After several weeks at Fourah Bay College, we left for the University of
Abidjan in the French-speaking Ivory Coast, again staying in the student
dorms and meeting many interesting college students.

Fishing village, West Africa

One of these was a young man who had spent a summer working in a
youth camp in Connecticut, and he told me the story about taking a train into
New York City and getting off on the wrong side of Central Park. He then had
to walk through the park at night. He said, "I've lived in the jungle all my life
and never been afraid, but I was afraid that night!" I told him that he had every
right to be afraid, and that even people who lived there would be afraid.

Remains of slave-holding building on the beach of West Africa

Our African professors lectured in English, and we learned about how different the countries had been treated by the French as opposed to the English during the colonial days as well as during the fight for independence.

We had the same African cooks all the time we were there, and they all had faces that had been scarified, making them look very fierce, but by the time we left, everyone had made good friends with them, and I think some of the women would have liked to take these cooks home with them.

Last view of home before that long voyage away from their families

Nigeria

The University of Lagos, Nigeria, was our next educational experience, punctuated by the worst traffic jams in the world. We had wonderful lecturers, such as one man who was unearthing bronze artwork; he had slides of much of his work, and most of us realized that even he did not realize the importance of his work in the art world.

By then, I was coming to the realization that even though it had been invaded by Muslims and Christians, Africa has a respectable religion of its own, and most professors refer to it as the animist religion, which is ancestor worship. They believe that after people are born, they age, working their way up to being a respected elder and finally, at death, to an ancestor, or deity. I may have heard the term animist used in an anthropology class, but until I lived with it, I had no understanding of its importance in human history and the lives of so many living people.

An effigy representing an ancestor, where food is taken, symbolizing feeding ancestors

When animists eat, it is proper for them to pour or drop a bit of food on the ground, symbolically feeding their ancestors, and there frequently are effigies where you can take food also to symbolically feed your ancestors. It made me think of taking communion in the Christian Church, which also claims to be family oriented, but not quite in the same intensity as the animist. I certainly learned that it is time we all started respecting each others' religious beliefs, or the lack of belief.

Another thing that is common throughout Africa and goes back to the ancient Egyptians is the playing of the *Awari* game, or *Mangala* game, where large seeds, shells, or stones are passed around on a game board with hollows in it, until the objects are all distributed in a numerical winning order. This memory game followed the slaves to the New World, and there seems to be evidence of it being played over seven thousand years ago.

As we were going down the runway on the plane headed for Ghana, I noticed that the case with our passports was not on the floor of the plane in its usual place, and I notified the flight attendant, who notified the pilot, who stopped the plane just before takeoff. We skidded off the runway and returned to the airport to retrieve them. The pilot came on the intercom laughing, saying that we were returning to retrieve important documents for our special guests. A similar incident happened to me in the Caribbean years later, with a similar response from the pilot; some cultures just seem to take things in stride!

Ghana

The University of Science and Technology at Kumasi, Ghana, was our next residence, and this is where I really fell in love with African marketplaces. However, there it seemed that coal-burning steam engines went by the entrance, so I could only enter after stepping over hot coals dropped by passing steam locomotives.

Everyone was having clothes made there, and I had a suit made by a tailor who did not speak English. But the fellow in the neighboring stall interpreted for me, telling me, after I was measured, how much material to get for the "political" suit that I wanted. At this time in

West Africa there was a popular design for men's clothing that was called a "political" suit. With just a pair of scissors, a tape measure, and a hand-operated sewing machine, he made a beautiful suit with pockets sewn on the inside, and no one could figure out how he could possibly have accomplished that. You get to know people while haggling in the marketplace over the price of things, and I think that maybe that is why they do it.

The interpreter in front and the tailor in back

Some of our group decided to make the long journey by car and air to Ouagadougou in Upper Volta, but I decided to stay and enjoy the marketplace. They brought me back what I later learned were quite valuable pieces of African art, such as masks that had been used in religious ceremonies, and I later gave these to a new African art museum at home.

Adinkra cloth used often in grieving the dead

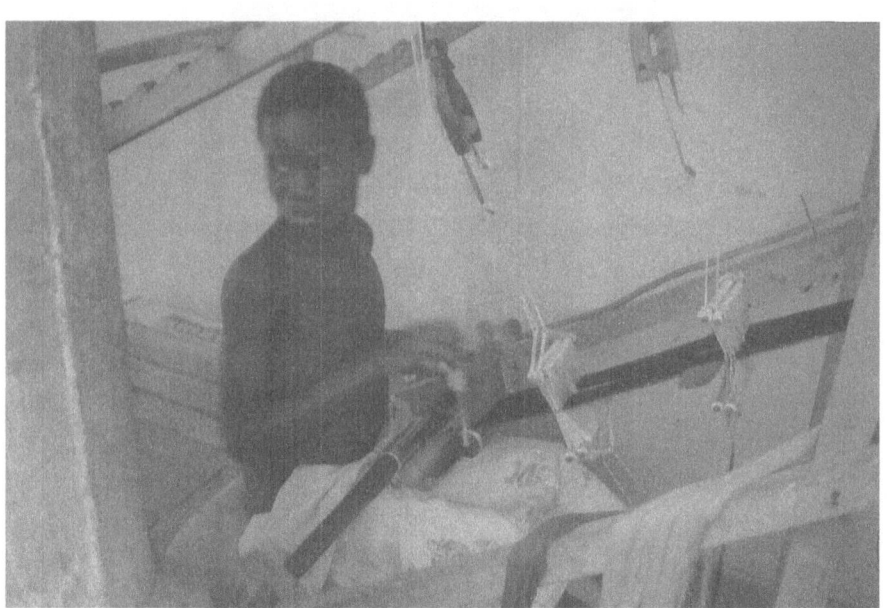

**Weaving Kente cloth, used mostly by the wealthy;
children learn to do this weaving at an early age.**

In Ghana, the ruler was the Asantehene, and we were honored to be one of the first groups to have an audience with him. He answered questions for us for about an hour. What a way to learn!

1971, Ghana, the Asantehene, or king

About five weeks into this study tour, we were having an evening meeting, mostly just reviewing what we had done and learned. Two married couples appeared to be extremely conservative, and both of the women began to cry. They began to tell how they had realized that they'd come on this tour expecting to confirm all the negative things they had always thought about Africa and Africans. They said that while they did not agree with polygamy, they now could see why it worked in Africa, and then came a profound statement that all four agreed on—and that was that they had all witnessed real love here in Africa.

We had a young black woman with us, and she had a scar on her cheek from a childhood fall. Wouldn't you know that we visited a village where a scar on the cheek, exactly like that one she had, was the tribal marking. In much of Africa, as with American Indians, their history is not written so it is referred to as oral history. Here in West Africa the oral history of many tribes tells about all the people that had been stolen away, saying that they would return someday. They all insisted that this was a sign that she belonged to this tribe, and that she should remain there with them in this village. However, when a person has been raised in one culture, it is hard to enter or return to another, so she did not think this was a good idea.

We had people of all races on this tour, including Asians, and we all chuckled when we entered a village and the chief greeted us by saying, "I see you are of many tribes!"

Dorothy

Dorothy was a tall, thin, attractive gray-haired woman whom we first saw in the airport in Los Angeles as the educational tour assembled. She was nearly eighty years old, and we all somewhat avoided her, thinking that we would probably have to carry her suitcase, and that she would be a drag on the tour. Well, not only was she not a drag, but she knew how to travel light, and she washed clothes out at night. Her favorite wash-and-wear item was a dress with a snakeskin print.

She told us the story of being on the SS *Andrea Doria* in 1956, and as it was sinking, she had to dive off in her nightgown. After she was rescued, someone asked what she needed, and she said a bra. Someone found one and offered it to her. She put it on and said it fit perfectly.

Because of the African religion's regard for the family and age, when our group visited a village and they saw this stately elderly woman, it was like Jesus Christ or one of his disciples entering a Christian church.

Our first day in Sierra Leone, when the teenage boys took me out in the ocean in a canoe, she had come swimming by us just like a young Olympic swimmer! She also took ballet classes regularly for exercise.

She had studied psychotherapy at the Jung Institute in Zurich, Switzerland, and would be stopping there on her way home from this trip. Having just read Janov's *The Primal Scream*, I was quite aware of how to detect neurotic behavior. One evening, Dorothy and I were talking, and she asked if I had noticed anything about the African people we were coming in contact with. I knew what she was going to say—that there was no evidence of mental illness or neurotic behavior, at least not in the countryside, where life was still lived in the traditional manner. The city people had pretty much taken on the white man's way of life, with all its faults.

Amsterdam, Holland

On my way home, I made a stop in Amsterdam, Holland, where a black friend was spending the summer working for an airline. I had brought handmade clothing that I had watched being made in different villages in West Africa, as well as beads and sandals, which I gave to him. The next day he wanted to wear as much as he could from his "homeland."

He put them on, and we went out to explore the city. At one point, we saw two young black men looking in a store window, so we stopped to see what they were looking at. All of a sudden, seeing the reflection of my friend in the window, one of the men turned and threw his arms around my friend, thinking he was from his village. I had gotten these clothes from his village in Ghana. He was there to become a medical doctor.

During the next few days, the four of us spent a lot of time together, and another spectacular educational experience took place getting to know people so different. What a coincidence!

Anne Frank

There in Amsterdam, we went to the place where Anne Frank wrote in her famous diary, and I felt that same overwhelming sadness that I had experienced above the *Arizona* in Pearl Harbor and going into the slave-holding dungeon at Bunce Island in Sierra Leone. All these atrocities seemed to have been perpetrated by sick, neurotic, power-hungry people with the desire to control other people. Ann Frank died when the war was all but over, but the memories she left will hopefully live on forever as a reminder of man's inhumanity to man, and perhaps keep reminding future generations not to let these atrocities happen again.

Each of these three places is associated with families feeling the enormous grief of losing loved ones, and again, as with the death of my cousin, I can hear Barber's "Adagio for Strings" playing in my mind, imparting a feeling of grief as it did in the movie *Platoon*. If you are not familiar with the music, it is worth Googling.

Chapter 15
More Traveling

The river

Over the years, we made many trips to the new place on the river, and there would be many changes, especially as family members passed on.

**Those who left us too soon: Cousin Jim (traffic accident),
Uncle Stan, and Dad (nicotine addiction)**

Mexico

In 1972, a friend who spoke some Spanish wanted to see a girl he had met in Tepic, Mexico, so we took the bus, Tres Estrellas de Oro, from Tijuana almost to the Guatemalan border, stopping in all the towns where there were interesting things to see. We spent a few days in each place, and he later married the girl from Tepic.

Riding buses in Mexico is a great way to travel and meet people, and it is quite cheap, as were the hotels we stayed in. The bus trip down from San Cristóbal de las Casas was especially memorable, with flowers sticking out the windows of the bus, chickens under the seats, animals strapped to the top, and children and baskets of food on people's laps. These were mostly indigenous Indians, and I felt almost privileged to be on the same bus with them, realizing that they were just plain good people, not needing wealth to feel happy. Everyone was equal on that trip down the mountain.

New York, Barbados, Grenada, Brazil, Peru

The next summer, I traveled with a friend that I had known since first grade, and our first stop was New York City. Every time we got on the shuttle from Grand Central to Time Square, he would ask, "Where are we going now?"

Then we were on our way to Barbados, and after arriving one evening, we were on our friend's balcony, which overlooked a Caribbean beach. They had fixed flying fish, a staple in the Bajan diet, and the houseboys were sucking out the eyes and consuming all but the lenses which they spit out. As the lenses clicked on the cement deck, I could tell by my friend's face that he was nauseated. He came over to me and said that his mother had not liked fish, and that he had never had a bite in his life. Well, that changed, as we had fish all three meals a days for the week in Barbados and for another week at Simeons' Guesthouse in Grenada.

Mr. Simeons is a black man retired from Shell Oil Company, and the guesthouse overlooks the beautiful bay. Guesthouses are fun because everyone staying there eats together family style. Grenada was getting its independence from Britain, and Mr. Simeons was so interested that he went to Parliament every day. The talk on the radio had to have been similar to what was being said when the United States was getting its independence.

Next we went to Rio de Janeiro, Brazil, where we hooked up with a friend of our friends in Barbados. He was a writer for the *Christian Science Monitor*, and he showed us around Rio. We visited Corcovado, Sugar Loaf, Copacabana, Ipanema, and many of the good restaurants. There is no other place on earth where you can see so many absolutely beautiful people so scantily clad than on the beaches of Rio, all smiling and many even posing for pictures!

We were then on a night flight from one of the most upbeat cities in the world to one of the most depressing, Lima, Peru. While it was frequently overcast, the people there produced many wonderful handicrafts, making it worthwhile to spend some time there.

The flight to Cusco the next morning was exciting, for we flew with snow-covered peaks on each side of the plane. The city of Cusco is quite a contrast to Lima.

The next morning, we headed for Machu Picchu. We boarded the train, which switches back and forth to get over the mountain. Going to the "Lost City of the Incas" was exciting, and upon arriving at the base of the steep mountain where the city is perched, we were informed that the buses up the mountain were not running. The only way to get to see this marvel of man's engineering was to climb on foot.

I have always carried too much weight, but the climb was worth it. The mountainside was covered with angel-wing begonias growing alongside baby orchids. I never would have imagined either of these growing in what should be a harsh climate.

Exploring all those stone buildings and wondering how those primitive peoples got all the stone up there reminded me that I had thought a similar thing in Egypt. They always seem to be laid out so scientifically, yet designed with religious meanings.

Returning to the train, we found many local Indians selling beautiful handicrafts, including unusual pottery, that I knew I could only buy there, so I did. I had learned in other countries that have an abundance of handmade items that you had better get them if you want them when you see them, as it is not likely that you will find them anywhere else.

Chapter 16
Building My House and More Traveling

U pon returning from traveling, I decided to complete plans for a house that I had designed for a hillside lot I had purchased at a reasonable price because it was on a steep hill with a steep bank in front and was considered almost unbuildable. Looking back, I wish that I had paid the thousand dollars more for the lot across the street that was on the downhill side, which meant that groceries could be taken directly from the garage into the kitchen, not up two and a half flights of stairs.

When we moved to La Mesa, there was a vacant lot next to our house, and in a few years, houses were being built on it. I've always been interested in how things work, and I would watch plumbers stand up the iron drainpipes and chink the jute into the fittings, then pour in the liquid lead to join the two. If the pipes could not be stood up, they would chink the joint with jute and then roll out clay and put it around the joint, forming a channel between the jute and the clay, then putting a doughnut at the top to pour the lead in.

It is much easier nowadays, as sewer drainpipes are plastic and put together with a quick-setting glue. Water pipes are usually copper and put together with solder, which is much easier than the old galvanized pipe where you had to cut the pipe to length, then thread each end.

When I was just sixteen years old, I watched our next-door neighbor put in a sprinkling system using galvanized pipe, and then I put one in our front yard, and I think it is being used to this day.

Later I learned to sweat the copper pipes together by watching a plumber put a water softening system in our house, and he took the time to show me just how to put the tip of the flaming torch at the right spot so the lead would suck around the joint.

I had taken several drafting classes in college, and I liked architecture, so I truly wanted to build a house that would be something that I had created. I always design things so they can be completed fast, and the law said that all I had to have was a kitchen sink and a working bathroom before I could move in. I moved in about six months after starting the work, finishing the inside while I was living there.

There were many problems, and I was only working on the house after work and on the weekends. There were several instances when I was tired and something was not going right, so I tried to force it, as was the case when a nail was stubborn and I hit it hard with the hammer, only to have water come gushing out of the wall. I had hit a water pipe. Another time, I hit wiring in the walls.

Building the house that I designed

I cut every board in the house, but I did have help carrying things up the hill, and even though I designed the place myself, I spent the next thirteen years remodeling it and adding on to it, also doing plumbing and electrical myself.

I had made some money on previous real estate, but generally I bought a load of lumber just as I could afford it, so the house was paid for when I was finished. Needing to have things paid for was caused by our family experiences of losing so much during the Depression.

Jerald and I (I am a single parent, never married) only moved from there because there was no place for my son to play, and if kids ran down the stairs, there was the chance that they would run out in the street in front of cars, which did happen to a neighbor boy about a month after we moved away.

1975 Caribbean trip

That year, I spent time in Barbados and then St. Lucia, where I heard one of the most wonderful Bach concerts performed in their old cathedral, with pipe organ, orchestra, and choirs from all over the island. What a treat.

Then on to St. Kitts and the wonderful ferry ride over to Nevis, watching the wide-sailing cargo boats, with black sailors in bathing suits up on the sides to keep the boat from tipping over. I was on the upper deck that was first class, and there was a high school soccer team in second class below. One of the Peace Corps teachers came up on deck and told me how great it was to teach on St. Kitts. I always met nice people on the interisland boats in those days.

It was my fortieth birthday when I left St. Kitts for Port-au-Prince, Haiti, arriving in the evening to stay in a guesthouse in an upper-class neighborhood, where all the wonderful French cuisine was prepared by a smiling thin black woman doing all the cooking on her knees in the backyard. She cooked on ceramic braziers, using charcoal for fuel, and the food was presented at a formal table as though it had been done in the most modern kitchen, and I don't think any of the other guests ever suspected where it had been prepared.

When she was not cooking, this same woman would go around to the front of the building, get a dishpan of water out of the swimming pool, and wash all the linens and towels for the facility, and she was always smiling.

Haiti was experiencing a drought at the time, and to get into the city I would take a tap-tap, a small truck with benches on each side of the bed in back for passengers to sit on. When a passenger wanted to get off they would tap on the back window and this is where the name came from. I made my way to a large cathedral built by slaves for the wealthy slave owners. It is hard to believe that this small nation accounted for about one-third of the wealth of France before the slave revolts and finally the formation of a nation in 1904. Enormous numbers of African slaves were brought here to provide cheap labor on the plantations growing coffee, sugar, cotton, indigo, and other moneymaking crops. I am sure there are wealthy families still living off family money that was made before the revolt.

As I walked up the steps to the cathedral, which was built in 1720, I could not believe my eyes. The doors were open, and I saw that this was where the starving people came to die. The floor was covered with the dying, and there was a baby that was just skin and bones, with distended stomach, lying next to its mother and trying to suck on a flat breast.

I looked up at the altar and thought to myself that this should be referred to as the "Dollar Altar." I could envision those wealthy plantation owners taking communion and being forgiven for their sins. The only reason that I can think of that religious leaders did not condemn the evils that were happening at that time is because they were part of this capitalistic venture and also making money.

I remember once when I was teaching junior high school and one of the black children told me that the reason black people were so bad was because the Bible said they were bad. Even the Bible has been used to psychologically destroy people, and we wonder why they have trouble learning.

Mixed in with all this, we still have all the so-called religious leaders who are still unable to distinguish right from wrong, like Pat Robertson, who says that the earthquake in Haiti was God's way of punishing the Haitians for destroying an evil moneymaking system. He tried to make the victims seem like the criminals. Too often, religion today is still being used to hide evil and transfer guilt from the guilty to the innocent.

I remember my black friend who grew up in Mississippi in the thirties, forties, and fifties saying that the only time he and his family felt safe was on Sunday morning, when all the Ku Klux Klanners were in church. It seems to me that of all the institutions that should be able to distinguish right from wrong, it is religious organizations, and if they can't, maybe it's time to think of them as just more capitalistic businesses, using the promise of heaven and the threat of hell to extort money out of people. If all they exist for is to create wealth for their leaders, maybe it is time to terminate their tax-exempt status and tax them like any other business.

After over two hundred years, the people of Haiti are still paying for overthrowing the white man and getting their freedom. For a long time, they have been mistreated by the outside world, with little trade, and they were left with nothing to cook with but the native trees, and they are nearly gone.

What do you do for fuel? In some places in India, I watched people scoop up cow dung and slap it on walls to dry to be used as cooking fuel, but in Haiti, there were only trees, and again, they are about gone. Capitalists still go to Haiti for the cheap labor but hardly make it worthwhile for the Haitians, as the pay is so low, and there are still so many problems, like how to generate electricity, acquire birth control, get fuel for transportation, and so on.

Instead of financially supporting bad dictators in these countries, our government could provide them with water and sewer systems, wind and solar power, and piers so goods can be delivered. All the places where slaves were left could use a little help, and it was the wealthy nations that created and benefited from these places, for hundreds of years, so helping them now doesn't seem too unreasonable.

Baggage problems

The summer of 1978, I left for New York, only to have my bag arrive several days later, and then I left for Rio, only to have my bag arrive later. The stay in Rio was different from the first, as I was alone and I realized that I don't like traveling alone.

One day I decided to go to Petropolis, a city in the mountains that had once been used by the ruling class where they had a summer palace. While standing in line at the bus depot, I met a nice Brazilian family in front of me. Their son was a college student who spoke English, and he decided that he would like to practice his English by spending the day showing me around Petropolis.

He took me to the Museu Imperial, where there is the gold quill that Princess Izabel used to liberate the slaves in 1888. In Brazil, a pen was used to end slavery instead of guns as was the case in the United States. The Civil War caused the enormous psychological damage that we still have to deal with to this day. The damage in the United States was also increased with the Jim Crow laws. There is evidence that while most wealthy slave owners in Brazil were married to European women, they also frequently had black mistresses, and the interesting thing about this is that the black family frequently inherited just as the white family did. In our schools we are still dealing with psychological problems that have been passed on generation after generation, caused by the Civil War.

We also went to the Santos Dumont House Museum, home to Alberto Santos-Dumont, who is the Brazilian father of aviation and also the inventor of the wristwatch. It seems as though the airplane was invented about the same time in three places—France, Brazil, and the United States—but Dumont was so distraught at how evil the airplane had been used in WWI that he committed suicide!

I once took the cable car up to the top of Sugar Loaf, only to arrive at the top and have the cable cars stop operating, and I realized why as the storm hit and there was wind and lightning all around me. My first thought was that I would not survive this ordeal, but like life in general, if you just stay calm in the bad times, they will soon be over with.

Without thinking, the day I was to leave for Barbados, I went to the outdoor marketplace and bought two large bags of garlic for my friends to use in their restaurant. I didn't think about this being against the law. I checked my bag, only to have it lost for the next three months. The airport in San Diego called to say my bag had arrived, and when I went to pick it up, I'm sure I smelled rotten garlic as I entered the airport. I got the bag and opened it, only to see that everything had been pilfered except the garlic, which was sprouting and rotting. I disposed of the suitcase in the nearest Dumpster.

Taking a black friend to Barbados

Almost every summer and during school vacation periods, I traveled for the next several years, and one incident that I remember was in 1980, when a well-educated black friend with two master's degrees traveled to Barbados with me. After being there a couple of days, he made the statement that being in this rather formal country where the majority was black was the first time in his life that he had felt normal.

Bajans are rather proud of their black heritage, and I remember one day talking to a local there, who looked white to me, and asking him if he was treated differently because he was white. He replied, "We all have a touch of the tar pot in us here!"

The summers of 1981 and 1982, I spent some time at the Kingston Park guesthouse on St. Vincent. This was an old plantation house that had been converted to a guesthouse, and the large lower floor had a nice dining room. While there in the summer of 1982, I sat next to a racially mixed couple—she was black, and he was white. They had brought their Jeep up from Union Island on the interisland barge for repairs, and they were getting ready to go back home. I told them that I had planned to go down that way on the barge in about two weeks, and I asked if there were any guesthouses there. She said, "No, but you can stay with us." I asked how much they charged, and she said that it was a dry island (not much rain), so I could just bring a bag of vegetables.

Two weeks passed, and early in the morning, I went to the local open-air marketplace. I bought a large bag of vegetables and boarded the WWII barge filled with local people, farm animals, sacks of feed, and a vehicle or two. I think we must have stopped on each of the Grenadine Islands belonging to St. Vincent, pulling up on the beaches and being met at each one by most of the inhabitants. At that time, the boat only came twice a week and this was the most exciting happening in their lives.

The barge arrived in the early evening on Union Island, and sure enough, there was the young black gal that I had met at the Kingston Park. Her first words were, "We were expecting you!" She introduced me to some of the Peace Corps people there at the landing, and then we headed up the mountain.

New friends where I stayed on Union Island in the Grenadines

Her husband's mother had bought the entire top of a hill and had an architect design three family houses in different locations there. She fixed dinner that evening, and I learned that she was a teacher, so we had lots to talk about. I had a nice downstairs room all to myself, and we had a good rain that night, which they needed.

The next morning after breakfast and good-byes, he put my suitcase on his head, and we started down the mountain to the airport, only to hear a large bang as we were walking. When we got to the field and the terminal, which consisted of some fellows playing cards in a small open-air building, we learned that a few minutes before a plane had landed and blown two tires. We could see it across the field in the bushes.

We asked if there was a plane to Grenada anytime soon, and one of the fellows at the table said that he would radio an airline and find out. There was one seat on a plane that only stopped there if there was a passenger, and he told them there was.

After a while, a small plane landed, and I got aboard, soon realizing that it seemed as though the others on the plane were dignitaries from other countries, but they were quite friendly, and upon landing, I arranged to stay at Simeons' Guesthouse.

Grenada under communist control

Mr. Bishop had gained power, and I was returning just before the United States invaded. Mr. Gairy was deposed and was living in San Diego, the US government still supporting him. The United States seems to support the bad ones and neglect the good ones.

Grenada's biggest problem was that for tourists to get from the World War II airport to the city of St. George's, the taxi had to travel quite a distance, over a volcano on a dirt road. Tourism was one of the few ways the island could earn money, so Mr. Bishop was trying to get a larger new airport near the city, where larger planes could land, bringing in more tourism. He asked the United States for money and was offered five thousand dollars, and he said that they couldn't build the toilets for that. It is strange that the United States did not offer more, as Grenada is a strategic island next to the island of Trinidad, which has oil and is one of the largest deposits of asphalt in the world. Mr. Bishop went to Cuba, and they did the right thing—instead of giving money, they sent men and machinery to build the airport.

It was interesting that there were no longer large numbers of policemen in St. George's, and you could go out at any time and feel safe. I even walked up to the door of the barracks where the Cubans were staying, and no one questioned me.

Almost daily, Mrs. Simeons gave me information about their communist revolution, and one day she asked if I wouldn't like to go over to Grand Anse Beach. I did, and as I was getting out of the car, there was a cute teenage girl nearby, and Mrs. Simeons introduced me to her, later mentioning that she was the prime minister's daughter.

I had been there almost two weeks when Mrs. Simeons asked if I wouldn't like to go to a program at the teachers college, and having nothing else to do, I said yes. I should have been suspicious when the guests for dinner were the prime minister's mother, sister, and daughter; the prime minister would have been there, but he was in the United States on business.

After dinner, we got in cars, and when we got to the college and walked to where the program was, I noticed a uniformed guard at the door. He opened the door wide as we approached, and there was the entire front row waiting for us. Flashbulbs were going off, and I tried to cover my face, realizing by the flags and decorations that this was a communist meeting. The entire crowd was singing the Cuban national anthem and my only thought was that I would never be let back into the United States.

My next stop was in Barbados, and I gave all the communist propaganda to a friend who worked in the archives in Barbados. He said they were glad to get things like that. I did make it back into the United States without any trouble.

Just a few years ago, I talked with a young doctor from Granada, and he indicated that most people in Grenada felt that the United States was responsible for the assassination of Prime Minister Bishop, and that the invasion was just to get President Reagan reelected. It is strange to me how the United States could support a tyrant like Gairy, who was essentially a dictator, and not Bishop, who seemed like a good person.

Chapter 17
Adopting My Son and More Family Times

In 1980, I decided to start the process of adopting a child, contacting the San Diego County Department of Adoptions and going through interviews. I started the nine-week program where they study you and you study yourself, deciding if you should adopt. You also examine your qualifications, what type of child you can handle, and so forth. I joined a fathers' group that they recommended, some had already adopted and were planning to adopt again, and I met a lot of great people and learned a lot about what to expect in the process, as well as what to expect after a placement.

Adopting Jerald

After two years of going through the adoptive process, at the end of the summer that had been spent in the islands, I received a call that there was a six-year-old black child available, and I could visit the foster home and meet him. I learned later that a black social worker had placed him in a white foster home because he had been so abused by black women that he would get very emotional in their presence.

In the adoptive process, I had decided that my only consideration was that the child be young, not a baby but not a teenager, and race was not a factor for me. Having traveled so much and gained so much respect for all people, race was of little importance. Children are children. He came to visit several times and was placed just before Christmas in 1982.

Almost losing Jerald

During the adoptive process, in the fathers' group a social worker met with us on a monthly basis. He was working on his doctoral degree and the subject of his thesis was single-parent adoptions. The local newspapers had contacted him about doing an article on this subject, and he asked if the paper could contact about three of us. A reporter came to our house for an interview and took a picture of Jerald on my lap, and this large photo appeared on the front page of the local paper.

At this time, the chief of Social Services was a young black man, and this was the first he knew that his social workers were doing interracial placements. He went ballistic! My social worker called and said that he wanted the child returned immediately. My family and I had already fallen in love with Jerald, and race had never been an issue with anyone in the family. I would have been the first to say that in most cases, children should be placed with parents that most identify with them. In this case, I had so much experience with many different races and cultures, and Jerald had such a negative experience with black people, that it seemed best for him to stay with me, where he was doing very well. He had been through too many failed placements and bad experiences, and to have another failure would have been detrimental to him. An example of the confusion in his life is evidenced in the fact that when I got him in the first grade, my last name made the fourth last name on the school records for that year!

I got a lawyer, and we started the battle, which was to culminate in a hearing by a local private adoption agency. In the meantime, my father, who was very fond of Jerald and looking forward to Little League with him (he had already taken him to get his mitt), had a heart attack. He died a day or so before the hearing, and the last words he said to me were, "Have they taken Jerald yet?" Dad loved baseball and would play any chance he got, and after Jerald came, he said very proudly that he had substituted as a catcher for the Negro League once and had caught

Satchel Paige. There had probably been a time when he hadn't been proud of this, but he was then.

At the hearing, the judge ruled in my favor, but within the next day or so, The Department of Social Services filed in court, saying that I was a pedophile and was already molesting Jerald. The judge wanted all the lawyers, district attorneys, and Jerald and me there the next morning before court started. We were all there in the hall outside the courtroom, and Jerald looked at me and asked what was going on in the room, so I picked him up, and he looked through the little window in the door and began smiling and waving. I did not know at the time that he was waving at the judge! A few minutes later, the bailiff came to the door and said that the judge wanted everyone but Jerald and me in the courtroom.

My lawyer came out smiling and wanted to talk to me alone, and he said that the judge had gotten mad and said that they all must have thought that he had just fallen off the turnip wagon. He said that no child that was being molested would be smiling and waving in his molester's arms, and that they were never to pull a stunt like that on him again.

It was just a few days later that they found another judge and tried a new angle, and this went from judge to judge for several months before going to the appellate court, where nothing can remain confidential. The entire case was in the news. Because Jerald was actually under the control of a juvenile court judge, we had to appear before him, and he was so disgusted with what was happening that he took Jerald away from the Department of Social Services and placed him with the Juvenile Probation Department. He ordered a complete investigation of me and the whole case, and when this was done, he said that it was the finest report he had ever read. In the meantime, they were still trying to destroy my character in any way they could, and we were back in the appellate court again, where they again found in my favor, so then they took the case to the California Supreme Court, where Chief Justice Rose Bird ruled in my favor. The next day, we were back in the juvenile court with the judge that had removed Jerald from control of the Department of Social Services, and there was the chief of Social Services in the courtroom. They were still trying to take Jerald. The judge listened for over an hour, but about the only thing the chief of the Department of Social Services could come up with was that this was the first time he had thought something was so important that it necessitated him coming to court. With the history of race relations in this country, I guess that he could not understand how a white family could love and nurture a black child and in many instances he probably would have been right. Every day of the last year of my mother's life she would call to ask how Jerald was and to tell him how much she loved him.

Finally, the judge said that this had gone on for a year and a half, and no one had come up with any reason why I could not be a good father—and why this was not a good placement for Jerald. He said that it was all over, and we were going back in his chambers to complete this adoption now!

Jerald visits on Thanksgiving 1982, Grandma ("Mom"), me, Jerald

For about the first eight months after Jerald was placed with me there were signs of emotional problems, such as heavy breathing at night and wetting the bed, sometimes more than once a night. I would just get up, change the bedding, and tell him that boys sometimes had this problem— and that it would go away.

The first time we went to visit black friends, their tall dark daughter answered the door, and I looked around to see Jerald back in the car. He got over the fear of black people, but there were many other psychological problems that I am sure were caused by the extreme abuse that he had before he was placed with me.

His name was Jerald with a *J*, and I had learned that black people named their children unusual names so that it would be easier to find them after they had been sold during the slave days. One day, when Jerald was in high school, he was working in a computer store and was wearing a name tag. A black woman kept looking at him and even returned to the store another time. She finally asked him if he had been adopted. She then asked when his birthday was and ended up saying that she thought that he was her nephew!

We were invited to family gatherings and met Jerald's two younger brothers, who had been adopted by their mother's cousin. They would often come and spend weekends with us, and at first, I thought it would be good for Jerald to be close to his birth family, as I am quite a bit older. Then, about two years later, Jerald's mother showed up at the family Christmas party.

It turned out that every time she was in his presence, she would start drinking and smash him in the face with her fist, telling him that the reason she gave him up for adoption was that he was such a bad kid. He was three years old at the time she relinquished him, and all two- and three-year-olds are a handful, as anyone who has had a normal child knows!

Jerald's mother had been raised by her aunt's family, and her mother was dysfunctional. I am sure that this neurotic chain of behavior could be traced back to slavery and being taken from a loving family in Africa.

Jerald had learning problems, and I thought it was just dyslexia, which educators didn't know much about then, but he would later be diagnosed with ADD, dyslexia, clinical depression, and an eating disorder. He is a brilliant person, but he could seldom show it off in a formal educational setting, and so he acquired distrust for formal education, not contributing to any class.

Jerald feeding the deer at the river before the deck was enlarged

On the river, Jerald, Aunt Dot, and Uncle Bob at the controls

Jerald and my sister Janet at the river

This was never more evident than in 1986, when my mother, sister, Jerald, and I took the train to Oregon for my grandmother's birthday. After my grandmother's birthday, my sister would later fly to the Hall of Fame, and my mother would go by car with Uncle Bob, Aunt Monica, Grandma, and Aunt Dot. Jerald and I went on by train to visit other relatives in Portland, Oregon, and then by train across the northern plains. One evening, while in the club car of the train, with lightning flashing all around, Jerald and the other children all screamed when the lightning struck close.

In Chicago, we visited the Field Museum, the Shedd Aquarium, and the top of the Sears Tower, and then we flew to Albany, New York, where a friend took us down to Cooperstown, where Uncle Bob was being inducted into the Baseball Hall of Fame.

While at the Hall of Fame, Jerald spent a lot of time with Ted William's son and daughter in the hotel, and they all got autographs of former inductees before any of the people who had been in line for days.

1986, Uncle Bob giving his speech at the Hall of Fame

After leaving the Hall of Fame ceremonies my mother, Jerald, and I flew to Detroit to see the Ford Museum before continuing home.

Mother, Aunt Dot, Grandma, and Aunt Monica at the Hall of Fame

Ted Williams, Grandma ("Mom"), and Aunt Dot in the hotel at the Hall of Fame

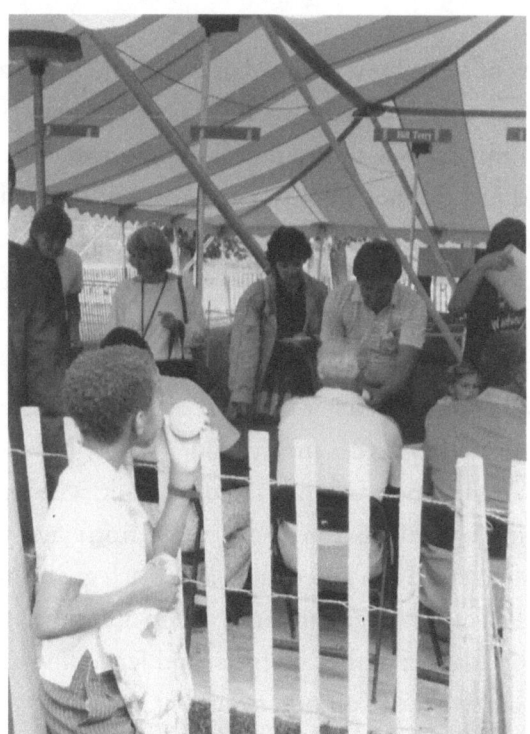

Uncle Bob signing autographs and, below, Jerald after getting autographs

Jerald at the Ford Museum

The first day of school after this eventful summer, when I went to pick Jerald up from school, the teacher said, "I'm sorry you weren't able to do anything this summer." When I told her what we had done, she could not believe it. Jerald just did not want to participate in show-and-tell. I think he was a little embarrassed at having a famous uncle.

Jerald was always good about calling if he was going to be late getting home, but one day when he was in high school, he did not arrive home at the usual time, and I began to worry, which you tend to do even more if your child is black. When he arrived home, just about dark, I started chewing him out, but knowing how to defuse me, he said, "I thought you would know I was just over at Argil's, and we went over to the park, where there were some black guys playing basketball. You know you've ruin't me; you've corrected my English so often that I can't even talk like a black guy!" I told him that he could learn to talk like a black guy anytime, and to next time just give me a call.

Manipulation is a tool of the powerless, and Jerald knows how to use it!

Jerald was crazy about computers, and at six years old, he wanted a computer instead of an electric train, and I kept getting him bigger and better computers all the time. We practically had a whole roomful of them, and there were always many of Jerald's friends at our house using them; some of his friends practically seemed to live with us.

Jerald's learning problems meant that he was in special education classes, which was hard on him, being as brilliant as he is, and having to go to the school where your dad teaches isn't that great either. In those days, teachers didn't know that much about ADD, ADHD, or dyslexia, and I am afraid more damage was done than good.

When the brain does not process written words, it would be better to just read to the person with the problem or have audiotapes, such as might be used with blind students, rather than have them sitting there looking at books they never could read. It is common for the brain to develop with age, and reading often improves. With Jerald, it was more like I had been. He could read, but it was so much work that the material had to be something that he was *extremely* interested in before he would make the effort. It seemed as though I was buying him a computer magazine about every other day, and he would start reading it before we got out of the store.

Jerald also had problems in classes where he could do excellent work, like in art, but he didn't hand in the work because he didn't think it was good enough. I think he failed computers only because the teacher didn't believe that he could have done the kind of work he turned in. He did not pass enough classes to get a high school diploma, but he and a friend took computer classes at the local community college, and he got a job doing some 3-D animation. He had already made some money doing work for a TV station in Mexico.

In the evening, the company he was working for had a class for professional people to learn the LightWave program, and the teacher could not do this particular series of classes, so Jerald volunteered to teach the classes.

It turned out that a computer teacher from his high school signed up for the course, and when he realized who the teacher was, a special education kid who couldn't read and had not graduated from high school, he almost walked out. The day after the series of classes was over, he came to me and said that Jerald had been one of the best teachers he had ever had. That teacher has since gone on to work for Apple Computer, after designing classes for the high school based on what he had learned in the class taught by Jerald.

Jerald and one of his friends made demo tapes and had cards made, and they went to 3-D animation conventions and gave the materials out when they thought there was the possibility of employment. One day Jerald got a call from a company in Pasadena, saying that they had a project that had been botched, and that they felt he could clean it up. They offered him the job at the equivalent of seventy thousand a year and a furnished apartment for four months, when the project should be finished, which it was on a Friday—and the next Monday, he had a new job.

He learned a lot doing this, but he became burned out, as many do with sixteen-hour days and no weekends off, and with the birth of his son, his psychotically destructive past was catching up with him. Bouts with clinical depression would become more debilitating. Jerald is still having problems with depression, but he is a wonderful father and says that he is not going to let what happened to him happen to his son. Hopefully, this might end the neurotic chain that I'm sure can be traced back to Africa and the trauma of being torn from loving families. I could not have received a finer son.

Many more good family times at the river

Jerald's family: Ivonne, Jerald, and my grandson, Darius

Coloring Easter eggs at the river

Hunting Easter eggs at the river

Family on the deck at the river

Another time with family on the deck at the river

Chapter 18
Getting to Know Some of My Former Teachers

Some of my high school teachers: Gene, Eckoe, and Dorothy

G ene taught Spanish, and later, when I returned to teach at Grossmont, he confided that he had never had a Spanish class himself. He was a graduate of Stanford University and was fluent in Latin, and he said that with his background in languages, it was easy to teach Spanish.

Eckoe was my sophomore English teacher who helped me write the poem after the death of my cousin Virginia. At her memorial service, I expressed my gratitude for all that she had done for me.

At the very first teachers' meeting after I returned to teach, she told me that there is one thing you *must* do the first day of classes, because you will be too busy to do it later, and that is to learn all your students' names.

Dorothy Smith was the only college prep English teacher, and did she have a reputation … You did everything you could to avoid taking her class, but she was the only teacher teaching the class. She worked you to death while you had her, but you loved her after you were done. It was in her class that I gave the speech on automatic transmissions, and I think she thought I was more academic than I was because I was the only one to raise my hand and answered correctly what onomatopoeia is.

As good as my memory is for remembering my past, I have a hard time remembering which is the verb and which is the noun with the words *affect* and *effect*. For some reason, I do remember what a gerund phrase is, and when I was in the army working in technical writing, I remember some of the higher-ups trying to tell a technical writer that a sentence was grammatically wrong. I overheard them and told them it was correct. I always had my English grammar book on my desk, and I showed them that it was a gerund phrase and was accurate. A gerund is using a verb as a noun, such as "Running is fun."

Dorothy was also one of the originators of our famous Christmas pageant, and she put on the beards and mustaches for the performers and I was in the pageant for two years. That is where I began to know her. Her husband, Andy, was also a teacher there, but he had a stroke and was in a nursing home. She would leave school, pick him up, fix him dinner, take him back to the home, and grade papers until well after midnight almost every night.

When she was about ninety years old, she had a massive stroke and was unconscious for a while in the hospital; then she was moved to a nursing home. Helping clean out her apartment, I found a small book that she had written and bound, titled *What It Was Like to Teach at Grossmont High School*. Then I found the outline and the rough draft for her book. We all thought she would have just whipped the work out, but no, in her rough draft, she had put a word above and below almost every word, deciding later which would be best!

Dorothy also carved a linoleum block and wrote a verse for her Christmas cards every year, and I found the blocks and verses while cleaning out her apartment. I printed the blocks and verses on both sides of a legal size page and wrote a note telling her friends what had happened to her, and why they would not get their usual card. I think I sent almost two hundred of these out, and they were later used at her memorial service.

I went to visit her every Wednesday evening, often taking friends of hers, and for about a year, she did not remember that she had been a teacher. She would ask where all her friends were, and I would have to tell her that she was over ninety years old, and that most of them were gone.

All those Wednesday evenings for a year and a half I would go, and though we would talk, mostly I just held her hand, and I thought that it was interesting that with all the destruction the stroke had caused, she always smiled and remembered my name.

Then the evening came when I arrived and took her hand but got no squeeze in return. Her eyes did not open.

Summary

I knew that I have had an exceptional life, but it wasn't until putting it on paper that it all came together, and I realize that I have had some unusual experiences that have caused me to develop some perhaps unusual conclusions about people, life, and learning experiences.

My family was and is the most important thing in my life, and should be in everyone's life, and then there were life-changing experiences, some bad but mostly good. Some of these experiences were with people, and some were with places and things, but they all went into developing a full and rewarding life.

In his book *The Teammates*, David Halberstam describes how wonderful my grandparents were, and how this goodness affected my uncle Bobby Doerr. Again, his parents, my grandparents, were always known as "Pop" and "Mom," and their headstones are marked in this way; they seemed to be a father and mother to everyone.

Mr. Halverstam calls his book a portrait of a friendship. It actually is a psychological study of the effect four families had on their four sons who became major league baseball players. One of them was Ted Williams, who made it in spite of his dysfunctional family and abusive childhood.

The book is about two of the teammates, Dom DiMaggio and Johnny Pesky, traveling to see their famous friend Ted for the last time, for he was dying. My uncle Bob could not go because his wife, Aunt Monica, had suffered for a long time from the effects of multiple sclerosis, and in recent years, strokes had left her with only the use of her left arm, and she was unable to speak.

In the book, the trip is almost secondary to the psychological effects their families had on them while growing up. The reader becomes painfully aware of how Ted William's family caused him and his brother so much emotional pain. Ted escaped into the more acceptable form of relief by immersing himself in baseball and then fortune and fame. His younger brother was not so lucky, and the pain turned into revolt against society's rules. He spent a good part of his life in prison. I have concluded that the avenues of escape can take many directions, some positive and socially acceptable, and some destructive and not acceptable.

Ted's father and mother both had symptoms of emotional pain, or what is usually termed neurosis or psychosis. His father turned to alcohol and his mother to religion for relief. His parents were so consumed with treating their own psychological needs that they were not able to provide their sons with the love, attention, and sense of belonging that all children need. Frequently, this trauma leads to neuroses that may be harmful to learning. Sometimes love is replaced with material things, the love substitutes that support a capitalistic society.

When parents have emotional pain, they usually pass it along to their children because they are so consumed with escaping their own pain. Parents with emotional pain frequently add to the pain of their children by being physically and psychologically abusive, and then on top of that, they are frequently an embarrassment.

Other examples of famous people who "made it" in spite of childhood abuse are Oprah Winfrey and Marilyn Monroe, women who had been abused as children and then went on to fame and fortune. All too often, girls are sexually abused by what is supposed to be a loved one. Parents and loved ones are supposed to protect children from harm, both physical and emotional. The pain from these acts lasts for life. Therapy usually only helps a person live with the pain and find relief in positive ways. These two women both tried to escape the psychological pain with fame and fortune, but there were other behaviors that were not so positive, such as escaping with sex in the case of Marilyn and compulsive eating with Oprah. The problems were much more complicated and destructive than I have portrayed, even ending in the death of Marilyn.

Distorted logic might assume that because these women became famous and wealthy, all women should be sexually abused if we want them to be famous and wealthy. (I can just hear Oprah now, saying, "Oh my God!") Politicians seem to use this kind of logic quite often.

Every person is affected differently by his experiences, and most women, and to a slightly lesser degree men, are so destroyed by sexual abuse that they have a lifetime of problems and sometimes even need to be hospitalized.

The effects of emotional pain on learning are different for each individual; there is no scientific logic. Sometimes psychological pain produces fame and fortune—other times, a life of failure. In education, psychological pain, or low self-esteem, can cause a child to excel or fail.

There is no doubt in my mind that psychological pain can cause learning disabilities. I have also concluded that we all are the product of what we inherit through our DNA, our family histories, our life experiences that affect our psychological makeup, and the environmental exposure that we encounter through pollution. I especially believe that the idea of learning problems being passed on through DNA is quite likely.

I have spent most of my life working with people, especially children, and I have been interested in how family, life experiences, and traumas associated with these encounters, along with exposure to chemicals, may affect learning.

There is no doubt in my mind that my family is what helped me overcome and deal with my learning disability, and that many children nowadays do not have this luxury.

When there have been holidays or birthdays where the family in southern California could not travel to Oregon to be with the rest of the family, we would all get together in southern California. My sister Sharon, who died young with ovarian cancer, had two children, Craig and Linda. Craig had three children, Chad, Natalie, and Luke, and Linda had three children Jessica, Jake, and James. With my sister Janet, the families above, my son Jerald's family and me, we have regular large family gathering down south.

With any relationships there must be priorities and so it is with families and if the family is valued it must come first and so differences in religion and politics must be avoided or handed very diplomatically. I believe that this is one of the things that has kept our family so close all of these years; we just don't let petty differences get in the way of family love.

Part III

Capitalism and Why Children Don't Learn

Introduction

Regulated capitalism seems to be consistent with modern American values, but when capitalism is not controlled the system seems to revert back to where it started and to a near master-and-slave system. The rich get richer and the poor get poorer.

We still seem to have the remnants of the master-slave system to this day, with the Republican Party protecting the wealthy, the masters, and insisting that *they* earned the money, and the Democratic Party saying that it is the worker, the slaves, that earned the wealth, and that they should receive a fair share of the wealth. In any case, the system has a negative effect on children and learning, as I hope to show.

The Industrial Revolution added a new dimension of pollution, with even more destruction to children and learning. With all these events came the degrading of human life, which affects children, and I feel that it adversely affects their learning to this day.

Students are the by-product of capitalism
With the knowledge of my life experiences, which included thirty-five years of teaching in quite a variety of public school positions, it should be understandable how and why I have come to some of the conclusions that I have. I would like to present some of the factors that may cause children to have learning problems. These causes seem to be by-products of capitalism,

and they are getting worse all the time, but sadly, most of the critics of public education have never taught in the public schools, and they are therefore not qualified to make judgments in this area. Hopefully, I can help the reader understand some of the problems, how they were and are being caused, and give some ideas on solving or at least improving the problems.

I certainly am not an expert in this area, but the evils of socialism are usually quite overt, easily identifiable and in your face. The evils of capitalism come from trying to meet those needs of capitalism that I will identify. Meeting these needs frequently produces conditions that do not support learning, and I will try to show how capitalism uses or abuses these. They are in the use of the environment, psychology, sociology, and life experiences, and I hope they show how these problem areas affect the family, mainly children and their learning.

After writing most of this work about three years ago, I then left it for quite a while, until recently, when I realized that scientific research was beginning to back up what I had come to believe, based on my life experiences.

I have considered introducing the word *some* into the title, Capitalism And Why *Some* Children Don't Learn. The problem is that if a teacher has just one student in a class with a discipline problem or a learning problem, all of the students in the class will have a learning problem. This takes place because the teacher must spend more time with these students, thus taking away from the entire class, so all of the students have loss of learning.

Terms

Dr. Arthur Janov, in his book *The Primal Scream*, describes in layman's language what neuroses are, and what the probable causes are, and I would recommend his book as essential reading for anyone interested in this field. His thesis is that both physical and psychological ailments can be linked to early trauma in a child's life. He says that neuroses cause debilitating medical problems such as depression, anxiety, insomnia, alcoholism, drug addiction, heart disease, and many other serious diseases and compulsions, such as eating and sexual disorders. He also concluded that neurotics pass on neurotic behaviors.

I use the terms "emotional pain" and "psychological pain" instead of a raft of other technical terms to describe mental disorders or neuroses. I usually think of emotional pain as being temporary, perhaps caused by losing a friend, losing a job, or being in a minor auto accident. These things might affect learning for a short time.

Lack of love and attention and the effects of abuse are most often the causes of psychological pain, especially at an early age. We know from the example of Oprah and Marilyn how to cause psychological damage in women: just let them be raped by their fathers, brothers, uncles, or anyone, for that matter. Parents must protect their children from situations that might cause psychological harm, especially at young ages. I think of "psychological pain" as being more permanent and maybe affecting learning for a long time, if not permanently.

It is my belief that in order to develop psychologically, a sense of belonging needs to begin at birth, with closeness to the mother, and breast-feeding is a good beginning. The next step only takes place nowadays in what we think of as "primitive" societies, where the child is in constant touch with his or her mother, on her back, getting the sense of security and belonging. The next step is belonging to the family, the community, the church, the school, and so on.

At this time in our society, this neurotic chain can be traced back many hundreds of years, and its beginning usually starts with an unloving act.

There is the possibility that we are witnessing the slow disintegration of capitalism at this time, as capitalism's needs are getting much harder to satisfy. I have concluded that capitalism must have a list of conditions in order to flourish. Some of these needs are running out, some are getting expensive, and some, like being able to pollute at will, have just become too adverse to people's health and the general health of the environment. In one way or another, each of these needs has had the side effect of causing learning problems in children.

Chapter 19
Capitalist Needs Produce Negative Products

Money is the drug of choice for capitalists, and in order to maximize their dose, the following conditions typically apply:

1. They need a large quantity of *cheap* raw materials. In many cases we are running out of these.

2. They need a large quantity of *cheap* energy. Other countries are demanding their fair share of the world's supply of energy, so energy of all kinds is getting more expensive.

3. They need a large quantity of *cheap* labor. Slavery is no longer acceptable, and if wages are too low for too many people, there is no one to buy the products that capitalism produces. This is what brought about slavery and has now been replaced by labor from Mexico, China, India, and so on.

4. They need a large number of *neurotic, compulsive consumers* capable of purchasing the goods produced by capitalism. There is a vicious circle here; I feel that capitalism has been responsible for the creation of most neurotics and all the accompanying problems, so they are creating their own clientele.

5. Capitalism wants *no regulations*; they get in the way of profits. (There is the need to pollute without being responsible for the cost of cleanup.) Disposing of trash and the cleanup of by-products and chemicals that pollute the land, rivers, lakes, oceans, and air are things that capitalists want socialized. And when people are used up and are no longer needed they become human rubble and are just left to fend for themselves, often with few resources to fend with. It has been my experience that this human rubble passes along psychological problems that affect learning in today's students.

6. With capitalism, there is *no overall national plan*; anything goes when it comes to making money, with no regard for what is best for people or the long term of the nation. The tearing up of our electric rail transportation systems and putting this traffic on highways is a good example of this. The rest of the world has high-speed economical public transportation, but the auto industry and the oil companies in the United States still control transportation, so we are left with polluting, wasteful transportation systems that have turned our cities into parking structures, and highways into parking lots, while filling our air, water, and land with pollutants. These pollutants may be part of the reason children don't learn.

7. Capitalists *seldom take responsibility for the pollution* they create, chemical, environmental, human rubble (slavery is an example along with wages that are too low to live on), etc. The talking points of capitalists are that the minimum wage should be lower, and the rich should pay lower taxes.

For over fifty years, I have watched politicians, educators, religious leaders, and talk show hosts, to name a few, blame bad teachers and bad schools for children not learning. The children are not learning, and it is time to start examining these children in order to find the cause and make changes.

I believe that one of the reasons this has not happened is because the truth would point the finger at hundreds of years of actions by capitalists, and they don't want the expense of cleaning up the messes they have caused anyplace, including in our families and with our children and their learning. The government, or "socialism," is expected to clean up the pollution and human rubble caused by the capitalistic experiment!

The real dilemma is that democracy is easier to control by capitalists, but capitalists are not always favorable to education, because educated people are more likely to be thinkers and want more pay. The capitalist slave owners did not want slaves to be educated, because education gives people power and the ability to communicate and organize, and even today this scares capitalists.

Socialism seems to attract dictators who usually over control and take freedoms away from their subjects, so both systems need controls of one kind or another!

We should not equate democracy and capitalism, which some pundits like to do.

Socialism and communism are not the same thing, and there can be socialism without a dictator, and socialism can be controlled by democracy.

I am suggesting that hundreds of years of not properly regulating capitalism in the "needs" areas that I have stated above has produced the products that are listed below, and in one way or another, each item in the list below adversely affects the family, thus the children and their learning.

The United States is a capitalist Christian nation, and we should all be trying to find the causes for the items listed below. There is the possibility that the years of protecting the seven needs that I have stated above may have produced this list of destructive behaviors in the United States:

- We produced enormous psychological destruction with slavery and Jim Crow.
- We produced the largest genocide in the history of the world (Native American).
- We ended slavery with a destructive war.
- We have the largest military in the world.

- We have the highest per capita crime rate of any country.
- We have one of the highest divorce rates of any country.
- We have a high percentage of children in foster care (over 500,000).
- We have a high percentage of homeless people (over 600,000).
- We have an extremely high rate of drug addiction, perhaps the highest in the world.
- We have a high rate of poverty (35.9 million adults and 12.9 million children).
- We produce much more than our share of solid waste.
- We produce much more than our share of air, water, and land pollution.
- We produce huge numbers of veterans with war-related problems, probably the largest in the world.

This list could go on and on, and it would be just more evidence that there are problems that need solutions. We must begin by asking this question: *Why* is our nation first in so many negative areas? With just a little examination, each of the items above, and more, could be traced to capitalism's need for neurotics, and neurotics' needs or contributions in the above areas.

All the above products of capitalist needs have had and are still having a negative effect on our population because of the negative effects on the family, children, and their education. Once the psychological destruction is instituted, it starts the chain that gets passed on from generation to generation, and breaking this chain takes some pretty extreme events, and all along its "links," there is the likelihood that it will affect learning in our children.

Capitalism has created some great things, but it also seems to have a self-destructive quality. With some proper controls, the causes could be brought under control. Fixing the damages done over hundreds of years is going to take major social programs and educational programs. It will take more than just getting rid of bad teachers.

Chapter 20

Unregulated Needs Cause Environmental Pollutions That Cause Environmental Problems That Cause Learning Problems

C apitalism needs large quantities of cheap raw materials and does not want the expense of cleaning up the pollution they cause.

It took billions of years to create coal, oil, and gas on this earth, and in just a little over one hundred years, this chemical process has been reversed with the inevitable release of stored-up chemicals and energy that are now affecting our environment and learning.

Virtually everything we eat nowadays is filled with chemicals. Even most of our supposedly healthy vegetables are grown in chemicals or have been sprayed with them, and now we even have "engineered" foods with lots of salt, sugar, and fat added, almost making them addictive.

I read years ago that a family in an older area of Boston decided to grow some of their own vegetables along the side of their older home. They later found that the vegetables were filled with lead from the many years of peeling lead-based paint that had washed off the old house and into the soil.

Pesticides improve the yield and make more money, but they have been linked to learning problems as well as many health problems, and some examples of the use of pesticides and chemicals on our food include the following:

- Apples may have as many as thirty-six different pesticides used and absorbed into them.
- Blueberries have about fifty-two different pesticides.
- Celery has about twenty-one different chemicals.
- Bell peppers have forty chemicals.
- Tomatoes, canned—the lining of the can is toxic.
- Popcorn—the lining of the paper bag has toxic chemicals that can be released when microwaving.

These are just several of what should be considered healthy foods but which contain chemicals that we know can cause changes in human reproduction, damage to brains and nervous systems, including decreased intelligence, and increased attention problems in children.

Nowadays our school playgrounds and parks have artificial turf that contains ten times the amount of lead allowed under state and federal guidelines for children's products! Lead is known to affect the brain and learning, especially in young children, and for years, it was a gasoline additive injected into the air by the tons through auto exhaust. And for many years we took this lead into our bodies through our lungs, and of course, it has gotten into the food chain.

Nicotine, caffeine, and alcohol have long been taken into the body, and we are still finding negative affects from them. It has now been shown that secondhand smoke can be extremely detrimental to people, especially the young and developing fetus. Once a chemical gets into one's body, it usually has an effect on every cell in the body, including the reproductive cells, and the effect is not usually positive or temporary.

We eat fish from waters that have been polluted with mercury from years of coal-burning power plants putting out tons of chemicals, such as mercury. We know mercury affects the brain and learning, especially for the young and unborn.

We eat meats that have been injected with hormones, vaccines, and other chemicals. The meats and poultry that have been injected with hormones to make them fat are doing the same to us. We have no idea what these chemicals may be doing to our delicate brain cells, especially the brains of young children, but one thing we do know is that they help make a lot of capitalists monetarily fat while just making us physically fat!

This is only touching the surface of chemicals we take in that might have a direct effect on learning or may even affect future generations through the changing of genes, chromosomes, and DNA.

Children drink beverages filled with sugar, the "love substitute," which should be labeled a drug because of its extreme refinement and concentration. Those drinks frequently have other chemicals that are not nutritious and probably bad for us. Sometimes sugar alone may even cause behavioral problems in our students.

One of the saddest findings lately has been that mother's breast milk has the largest concentration of toxic chemicals, and cow's milk is probably not far behind. This has many ramifications because breast-feeding is the first unconditional love act, and bonding begins to take place with the new child. This is where the child gets his or her first sense of belonging, and it helps to keep the child from having a sense of rejection. Breast-feeding is a positive act, and combining it with a negative effect is a sad and serious problem.

The body seems to concentrate all chemicals in the mammary glands and doesn't distinguish between healthy nutrients and toxic chemicals. It is known that concentrations of chemicals can cause cancer, and this may explain the high rate of breast cancer in women. The body doesn't know the difference between nutritious chemicals and toxins, so it directs the bad chemicals as well as the nutrients to the breast tissue so that these tissues are constantly bathed in toxins!

Another example of neurotoxins being introduced to children is the use of brominated flame retardants (BFRs) in clothing, pajamas, and even the pillows they put their heads on. A known neurotoxin, BFR could affect learning, memory, attention, and behavior in children.

A child may sleep in an environment of BFR and get up in the morning to eat cereal out of a box that may have chemicals in the packaging, which has spread to the food inside so that a completely new chemical has been created. There is the possibility that none of the original chemicals were properly tested for neurotoxins that might affect children, let alone what the new combination might do.

In art, we learn to mix colors, and all students know that mixing some colors produces unsatisfying results, and mixing all the colors produces a muddy color that looks toxic. The same thing is done with tone colors in music, and some combinations of tones are good, while some combinations of notes are sour. I feel that we are now combining tones that are not good together, and which may even harm our hearing! Because we breathe in chemicals, ingest them, and they cover our skins, chemicals are being combined constantly, with no testing for toxicity or for harm to our bodies—whether our brains, nervous systems, or reproductive systems.

Dioxin is produced by burning many chemicals together. It is considered a *super toxin*, and we are all often breathing it or absorbing it. Books are now being written about toxins and their effect on people and learning.

Chemicals in our environment are there to make money for capitalism, or they are there as a waste product of capitalist manufacturing.

Neurotoxins

The Parents as Teachers organization produced a lot of information on *neurotoxins*, and in the following paragraphs, I paraphrase some of this information.

There is research telling us that exposure to neurotoxins such as lead, mercury, alcohol, nicotine, tobacco smoke, and some pesticides can affect the developing fetus and impair normal brain development. It is logical that this can result in learning and developmental disabilities. Everyone is vulnerable, but children, and most especially developing fetuses, are highly susceptible because their systems are still developing and growing and are more easily disrupted by toxic exposures.

There is evidence that more than half of all special education children in public schools in the United States have learning disabilities. ADD and

ADHD are on the rise. It has been found that exposure early in life to such neurotoxins, those chemicals that injure cells in the nervous system, such as *lead, mercury, alcohol, tobacco smoke, and some pesticides,* can lead to lifelong learning, behavioral, and developmental problems. There is a gradual accumulation of these chemicals, so these problems may show up slowly over a child's development.

Some of the symptoms that these neurotoxins may cause are:

- Compromised physical growth, vision problems, or hearing problems
- Hyperactivity
- Poor attention span
- Impulsiveness
- Noticeable learning difficulty
- Memory impairment
- Decreased intelligence (IQ)
- Mental retardation
- Speech or language difficulty
- Social immaturity
- Aggressiveness, irritability
- Sensory processing problems
- Poor motor coordination

Young children's typical behaviors promote exposure to toxins, such as putting hands in their mouths, mouthing dirty objects, and playing on the floor where allergens, such as dust and toxic chemicals, settle and collect. These behaviors are a crucial part of normal development and the way a young child learns.

Alcohol
According to the Surgeon General, no amount of alcohol consumption can be considered safe during pregnancy. Alcohol can damage a fetus at any stage of pregnancy and result in lifelong problems.

Fetal alcohol spectrum disorders (FASD) is a term describing a large range of effects that can occur in an individual whose mother drank alcohol during pregnancy. These effects may include physical, mental, behavioral, and/or learning disabilities. Fetal alcohol syndrome is a medical diagnosis of the severest form and includes learning disabilities, growth deficiencies, abnormal facial features, and central nervous system disorders.

When a pregnant woman drinks alcohol, her baby also drinks alcohol. Therefore, the risk of a baby being born with any of the fetal alcohol spectrum disorders increases with the amount of alcohol a pregnant woman drinks. Studies indicate that a baby could be affected by alcohol consumption within the earliest weeks after conception, even before a woman knows that she is pregnant. Again, there is no safe amount of alcohol for the mother to drink during pregnancy, and I believe that both men and women of childbearing age should refrain from the consumption of alcohol.

Lead

It is estimated that 10 percent of preschool children have lead levels that are high enough to cause learning disabilities. Children under six years are most at risk, and the most prevalent exposure to lead is from lead-based paint that was used for many years and is now deteriorating and entering the environment.

Lead poisoning may occur due to water pipes, lead-glazed pottery, vinyl mini blinds, lead solder in cans, hobby paint, stained glass, fishing sinkers, leaded gasoline, some costume jewelry, and some playground equipment.

Even at low levels, lead exposure can cause learning disabilities, IQ loss, and behavioral problems.

Mercury

Researchers have found that high levels of methyl mercury in the bloodstreams of unborn babies and young children may harm their developing nervous systems, making these children less able to think and learn.

Mercury is released into our air, land, and water by polluting industries such as coal-fired power plants. It is found in a wide variety of products and in the toxic form of methyl mercury in some fish. Other toxic exposure may result when an item containing mercury breaks, is thrown in a landfill, or is incinerated. Such items include thermometers, dental fillings, fluorescent light tubes, amalgam, thermostats, barometers, or alkaline batteries.

Tobacco

Smoking harms infants and young children by causing them to receive less oxygen. Lack of oxygen has been linked to less weight gain during pregnancy, miscarriage, and preterm labor. Smoking during pregnancy is related to 10 percent of all infant deaths.

Pesticides

Pesticides are toxic substances such as herbicides, insecticides, and fungicides, which are intended to kill or control weeds, insects, rodents, fungi, bacteria, and mildew. Some of these pesticides harm humans, and pesticides are found in products such as bug sprays, certain pressure-treated woods used to build play sets, and some waxes on fruits and vegetables.

Bhopal, India

In Bhopal, India, in 1984, forty metric tons of poisonous gas from a Union Carbide plant used to manufacture pesticides spewed fumes into the atmosphere, and it is estimated that as many as twenty thousand people have died because of this. More than six hundred thousand Indians have become ill or have had babies born with congenital defects over the past two and a half decades. Cleanup has never been done properly, and the groundwater over a large area has become contaminated. The US company that is responsible has still not taken care of the damages, which were caused by neglect and cost-cutting by the company. This is typical of capitalist companies. They want the government, with its regulation and rules, to stay out of their business but to be there later to clean up the mess!

Love Canal

Love Canal in New York State has twenty-two thousand tons of toxic waste, and children who live near there have arterial birth defects, deformed teeth, thyroid disease, pernicious anemia, ADHD, and many autoimmune conditions. Children whose parents lived there before the evacuation have double the risk for reproductive problems, low birth weights, preterm deliveries, and birth defects. They are also at risk for kidney, bladder, and lung cancer.

Thirty years after nine hundred families were evacuated, the area is still contaminated. No cleanup has been done, just a fence installed around the most contaminated area. Starting in the 1920s, the Hooker Chemical Company used the Love Canal as its dump site. In 1953, they sold the dump site to city officials for one dollar, and the deed warned of dangers, including a disclaimer against future liability.

An elementary school was built on the perimeter, and by 1978, about eight hundred houses and 240 low-income apartments were built near this dump site. Shortly after this, the water table began to rise, and toxins erupted in the backyards of the nearby homes.

The schoolyard was contaminated, and children would return from recess with sludge-covered clothing and blackened burns on their hands. Surveys have shown that 56 percent of the children had birth defects, and there was a 300 percent jump in miscarriages by women living in the area.

Occidental Petroleum was the parent company to Hooker Chemical, and they have paid $129 million for the mess, but it still has not been cleaned up, and it was learned of over thirty years ago.

The worst of it is that there are fourteen hundred other sites with similar problems in the United States!

Cuyahoga River in Cleveland, Ohio

In 1868, 1883, 1887, 1912, 1936, 1941, 1948, and 1952, the Cuyahoga River in Cleveland caught fire. In 1952, it caused $1.5 million in damage. Nothing could live in the river. It now has been cleaned up, but for over a hundred years, it was a toxic waste and groundwater around it was probably contaminated along with nearby drinking water wells.

Oil companies

Another example of potential pollution is that oil companies are not being held responsible for potential disaster. Since 1940, they have left twenty-seven thousand abandoned capped oil wells in the Gulf of Mexico, and no one monitors them to see if the pressure is regenerating or if the caps are deteriorating. This is a disaster waiting to happen, as thirty-five hundred have only been temporarily capped. They were supposed to be permanently capped, but the oil companies keep circumventing the laws.

Toxins and DNA

With new machines, scientists can study the brain, and with knowledge of DNA advancing rapidly, scientists are learning a great deal about how the brain works, and how chemicals and emotions affect it.

Every cell in a person's body is soaked in chemicals that have the potential to do harm, and that includes our reproductive cells, with the genes, chromosomes, and DNA possibly being altered. We should now be asking how these mechanisms might be permanently changed in both women and men. We usually like to blame women for most of the reproductive problems, but I think it will be found that men's DNA can be altered just as easily, and the likelihood of these changes being positive is very small.

There is a good possibility that scientific findings will confirm that learning disabilities can be caused by emotions that change our body chemistry, and these changes may be passed along through DNA. Moreover, this may have been taking place for many centuries and generations, culminating in the learning problems we are now experiencing.

Transportation and toxic chemicals

The reader may wonder what effect transportation can have on learning. It is not only a cause of chemical pollutions but also a sociological problem. Here in Southern California, where we have paved over almost all the land with freeways, you can go out daily and wipe your windshield with a paper towel, and it will be covered with a black greasy substance that is probably from the exhaust of cars, or the dust caused by brake wear, now known to contain copper particles, and copper is known to be extremely toxic. It is already known that copper causes serious neurological problems in fish and other animals, and we and our children are exposed to large quantities of *copper pollution* caused by vehicle brakes. This is especially bad in Southern California, with its enormous numbers of cars.

We are all breathing this in, and it is not only coating our lungs with the potential for disease, but our lungs are delivering these chemicals into our bloodstream. Since the lungs can deliver nicotine into the bloodstream, then it is likely that other chemicals may also pass that way. Once the chemicals are in the bloodstream, there is the potential for damage that could affect learning.

This copper from car brakes also is deposited on the highways and eventually gets washed into the waterways and finally into the food chain.

Copper is a known neurotoxin, and it has been introduced into the environment for many years!

Transportation causes environmental problems and social problems
In Southern California, many people spend more than two hours each way going to work, and that is four hours a day taken away from their children's needs, so time is a factor in the love affair with the automobile.

The stress of driving freeways also adds to the negative influence they have on all of our lives and this stress may be transferred to our children and cause stress in them that can affect learning.

For more than a half century, our roadways took more than forty thousand lives every year; this number has gone down in recent years, but many children still suffer the loss of a loved one or grow up with the trauma of not having a parent.

I worked at a school that was near a freeway, and not only did we get the chemical and dirt pollution, but the noise pollution was so bad that it made teaching and learning difficult.

At one time, Los Angeles had the world's largest all-electric interurban transportation system. Tracks went in all directions from downtown, through Hollywood and over the mountains to Canoga Park, to each of the beach cities as well as San Pedro and Long Beach. They went south to Huntington Beach, to Santa Anna and east to Riverside and Redlands.

That was the high-speed interurban system, and besides that, each city had its own electric system for local commutes. There was even a funeral car with stained glass that would come and get you at your house, pick up the body at the mortuary, go to the church for services, then take you to the cemetery for burial. You can still see one of these cars at the Paris Trolley Museum near Riverside California.

Freight was also transported over these lines at night when the tracks would not be transporting people. All this was done with electricity generated in one location where controlling pollution would be much easier than trying to control it in the thousands of individual vehicles on freeways. Private vehicles may not be kept in the best of working order so are much more likely to pollute.

Most of these systems were bought up in the late 1940s by General Motors, Goodyear Rubber, and Standard Oil Companies in order to install General Motors buses using Goodyear rubber tires, and each consuming gasoline or diesel oil produced by Standard Oil.

Freeways replaced most of these rail lines, and pollution got so bad in the 1950s that Los Angeles was known as the smog capital of the world. Often our freeways are parking lots, and our cities have more parking structures than office buildings, so air pollution is only one of the problems caused by the demise of electric transportation in many of our cities.

President Eisenhower owned a lot of stock in General Motors, and he was responsible for the interstate highway system; that spelled the near end of the passenger rail service in this country. Socializing the highway system is strange in that mostly private autos and trucks use them, and it would make more sense if fuel taxes paid for all highways. The federal government subsidizes highways by more than thirty billion dollars a year. In a capitalistic society, it would make much more sense to have public transportation socialized and private transportation take care of its own needs. The government is actually subsidizing private industry! *Most developed countries in the world know that rails are the most economical, least-polluting method of transporting people and goods.*

Here I will exaggerate a little just to get your attention. Essentially, four diesel engines on rails can move as many passengers or as much freight as one hundred engines in trucks or buses on highways. Those four diesel engines could be run on the used, filtered, cooking oil disposed of after use in all the eating establishments so prevalent in this country.

The demise of the railroads in the country set in motion the expansion of air travel, which is the most polluting, least economical form of transportation, as it takes enormous amounts of fuel to keep that tonnage in the air, let alone propel it to its destination

President Reagan caused the transportation problem to get worse when he lowered the mileage and pollution standards for trucks along with bumper standards and this started the epidemic of so many people driving big, inefficient, polluting SUV's.

All these actions caused *urban sprawl*, which causes most of us to drive too far and waste fuel and time, and the rest of the world added systems on to their electric rail transportation that are not nearly as wasteful as what capitalism has left us.

It will be almost impossible to undo all the harm, and keeping up with maintenance of a highway system and with heavy trucks using them; I believe it will bankrupt the country. Rails were made to carry heavy loads, and that is where the cargo on trucks belongs.

On 9/11, when all aircraft were grounded, the skies became a bright blue, and it became evident that air travel was responsible for an enormous amount of air pollution. The airline industry is also subsidized by over ten billion dollars a year by the federal government, and airplanes are one of the most polluting transportation machines!

Even if every chemical that we come in contact with was tested to be safe for humans, when we combine any of these, and there are many thousands, we get a new chemical that could be toxic! Coming into contact with one chemical is one thing, but we are all exposed to many thousands almost on a daily basis, and what they do to a child's developing body and nervous system is much more destructive than it is to an adult.

Chapter 21

Capitalistic Needs Produce Sociological Problems That Affect the Family, Children, and Learning

The need for cheap raw materials is one of the reasons capitalists took land from the American Indians, and the need for cheap labor is one of the reasons slavery was an institution and these two things are to this day affecting learning in our children. There are several examples of capitalism creating social problems: American Indians, African Americans, military, and low-wage earners.

I use American Indians and African Americans as examples often because I have some knowledge of these groups, as do most people, but anytime a child is not loved or is neglected or abused, the neurotic chain is likely to begin.

The military-industrial complex and their indiscriminate use of chemicals is one of the most alarming causes of learning problems, and the damages may even overshadow all of the other negative forces causing learning problems. Wars have been and are one of the most destructive forces in our country right from the beginning of the nation. Some times I think the damage may even be cumulative.

The American Indian and Genocide

When I was a child, movies portraying American Indians as the criminals were very popular, and no one stopped to think that the white man stealing his land was the real criminal act. This sold many movies, as it transferred guilt from the audience and their ancestors to American Indians, also giving them permission to keep abusing them. I would like to spend some time undoing the years of degradation of the American Indian.

In order to understand why some Indian children may have problems learning, it would be good to review some of their history. In an article by Guenter Lewy, he writes that according to Ward Churchill, a professor of ethnic studies at the University of Colorado, the reduction of the North American Indian population from an estimated 12 million in 1500 to barely 237,000 in 1900 represents a "vast genocide ... the most sustained on record." By the end of the nineteenth century, writes David E. Stannard, a historian at the University of Hawaii, Native Americans had undergone the "worst human holocaust the world had ever witnessed, roaring across two continents nonstop for four centuries and consuming the lives of countless tens of millions of people." In the judgment of Lenore A. Stiffarm and Phil Lane, Jr., "There can be no more monumental example of sustained genocide—certainly none involving a 'race' of people as broad and complex as this—anywhere in the annals of human history."

No wonder American Indians have a reputation for alcoholism, which only adds pain to an already nearly destroyed people, and this history of abuse is passed on from generation to generation, affecting learning even at this time.

There actually were three continents, North and South America as well as Africa, that had extremely similar and well-developed cultures. We like to think of their cultures as underdeveloped and the people not very intelligent, but my experience has convinced me that they were and are extremely intelligent, and their religious beliefs were greatly advanced. Their beliefs kept them in tune with God's creations, and it was a major part of their religion not to destroy that which God had created.

They frequently would ask forgiveness for taking the life of an animal, even when it was for food. They truly had an advanced culture and did not destroy the land, instead leaving it pretty much as they had found it and the way God had created it. All these people were essentially farmers, as described best in the *Guide to USDA Programs for American Indians and Alaska Natives.* Some information from this guide follows:

Indians were the first farmers in North America, and agriculture has been a mainstay of the American Indian culture and economy for thousands of years. In fact, the Indians of Central America and Mexico, or Mesoamerica, were engaged in agriculture seven thousand years before Europeans settled in the present-day United States.

Archaeological evidence indicates that American Indians began farming in what later became the continental United States by 5000 BC, utilizing indigenous agricultural practices as well as practices learned from Mexican and Central American cultures. By AD 1000, American Indian farmers had developed a productive and complex agricultural system based on corn, beans, and squash, which have been commonly referred to as the "three sisters." These American Indian farmers were primarily women; the men hunted and fished.

There had been variety in American Indian agriculture and economy before contact with the European civilization. American Indians in the northern United States cultivated the river valleys and flood plains with bone, wooden hoes, and digging sticks. American Indian women raised the traditional crops of beans, squash, and many varieties of corn—the most important crop. In the upper Great Lakes, the Ojibwa (Chippewa) and the Assiniboine sowed, harvested, dried, threshed, and stored wild rice. Some northern tribes also tapped sugar maple trees and made sugar. Over time, American Indian farmers in the southern United States cultivated squash and bottle gourds and then traded agricultural products in market centers. Southern farmers raised a significant amount of their own food as well as a surplus for lean times, and for trade with each other and later with the European settlers.

American Indians used highly developed agricultural methods and practices. The Southwest Indian farmers developed a new type of corn, which provided the subsistence basis for southwestern Indian civilization. They also cultivated several varieties of squash and beans, grew cotton, developed water conservation practices, and used several methods of irrigation. From AD 800 to 1400, the Hohokam Indians in the southwest, called the "canal builders," constructed major systems of irrigation canals that were 150 or more miles long. Although the Plains Indians relied mainly on hunting and gathering, by AD 1000, the Indians of the central plains practiced well-developed agriculture with corn, beans, squash, sunflowers, and tobacco being the important crops.

R. Douglas Hurt, writing on "The Native American Experience" in *American Agriculture: A Brief History*, wrote:

> *In retrospect, the history of Indian agriculture is the story of supreme achievement. Nearly three millennia before the arrival of white settlers, Native American farmers learned to cultivate plants of local and Mesoamerican origins. They discovered how to select the seeds that would yield maximum harvests in local soil and climatic conditions. By so doing, they made great strides toward farming in harmony with nature.*

When Hernando de Soto's expedition landed on the coast of Florida in 1539, his food supply was nearly depleted. American Indian agriculture was so bountiful that the Spaniards appropriated a three-month supply of corn from the fields, enabling the expedition to continue. The American Indian farmers later showed European settlers which plants to cultivate, particularly corn, beans, pumpkins, and tobacco, and how to make maple sugar and prepare hominy.

American Indian agriculture has had a significant effect on worldwide agriculture and economy. Jack Weatherford, in his book *Indian Givers: How the Indians of the Americas Transformed the World*, pointed out that Indians cultivated over three hundred food crops and contributed to the world three-fifths of the crops now in cultivation. The Indian farmers of North and South America gave the world corn, potatoes, sweet potatoes, tomatoes, beans, pumpkins, squash, chocolate, vanilla, papayas, persimmons, jicama, pecans, chilies, hickory nuts, peanuts, cassava, sunflower seeds, maple syrup, tapioca, and avocados.

American Indian agricultural crops have spread from American farmers to farmers in other parts of the world. Today corn is grown almost all over the world. The white potato spread from Bolivia and Peru to Ireland and across Europe to Russia, providing more calories and nutrition per acre than any grain. Corn and cassava contributed to the increase in Africa's population in the last century and throughout this century. Sweet potato and corn were cultivated in areas in Asia where rice did not grow. Clearly, American Indians' historic agricultural achievements made important contributions to the United States and the world.

Taking the land from the America Indians provided capitalism with the cheap land and natural resources that it needed.

The unanswered question is why genocide was used on such a culture. Not only were they physically destroyed, but their culture and religion were diminished to the point of being negated. The psychological destruction was enormous, and to this day causes learning disabilities for many of the people whose ancestors where subjected to the enormous trauma of having loved ones being taken away and their land confiscated and too often families being destroyed.

Psychological destruction is the first link in the chain, and each generation has the potential of passing it along, and in our schools today, we are dealing with the problems that started many years ago.

There is a cry for the Ten Commandments to be displayed in public places, but we still celebrate Christopher Columbus Day, and he was responsible for *killing* large numbers of people. There seems to be some inconstancy here!

Where were so many of the church leaders while all this was taking place? If church leaders cannot distinguish between right and wrong, to whom do we look?

Should the Irish potato actually be called the American Indian potato?

Slavery

Capitalism's need for cheap labor created slavery, with all of its social problems, and the capitalists' solution was to have a civil war, which made even more money for capitalists.

The need for cheap labor caused people from Africa to be brought to many places to make money for the capitalists, and when the land was worn out, the capitalists did not return these people to where they had gotten them. This created some of the worst problems in the Caribbean Islands, where recsources are finite. A good example of this is in Haiti, where large numbers of people were left with little resources to live on.

Half of the world still cooks with wood, and on Haiti, there is little wood left. This is just one of the problems on these islands. Population is a problem, for birth control is not always available, and the islands have only so much land and resources. This was left as someone else's problem to solve, and unfortunately, many of the problems we have today were the result of our forefathers' monetary gain. North America, South America, Central America, and the Caribbean Islands are still suffering from this capitalistic venture, and someone else is left with solving the problem, while I am sure there are still families enjoying the wealth from this destructive venture.

I have visited Haiti several times, and in 1975, they were having a drought. I stood at the entrance to the large cathedral in Port-au-Prince, looking in at the floors completely covered with people starving to death. The church had been built with slave labor for the aristocracy when Haiti was one of the wealth-producing places in the world, importing approximately fifty thousand African slaves a year to satisfy this capitalistic venture and the need for cheap labor.

The neurotic needs of the European plantation owners were met with the wealth gained from cotton and sugar, but in the process of gaining wealth, their treatment of people was transferring their neuroses to the people being used and mistreated.

We know that religion was important to these wealthy plantation owners, and there had to have been a lot of them because the cathedral is enormous, but why didn't the church recognize the evils of slavery that surrounded it and even used it? Even today, religion and the church are often used to transfer guilt from the guilty to the victims!

Haitian slaves revolted and took over the land, and the capitalistic world has been punishing and using them ever since. The United States obtained the Louisiana Purchase because of the problems in Haiti. The United States then had more land and natural resources to meet its capitalistic needs.

Haiti is an example of capitalism's worst nightmare, and that is the loss of cheap labor, which is what happened with this enormous slave revolt that was responsible for the loss of about one-third of France's wealth as well as its sale of the Louisiana Purchase to the United States.

This also resulted in the abuse of the Native American Indians in this territory. Both of the groups are still paying for these acts in history, and teachers in the classrooms have to deal with the problems that this capitalist venture caused, and which have been passed down from one generation to the next.

Haitians are good people and don't deserve what has been done to them.

African Americans and slavery

Slavery in the United States was enormously destructive, and Jim Crow Laws helped make the white man into the victim and the African American into the criminal, and of course, criminals are hanged (lynched) and criminals certainly couldn't sit next to a white person in a movie theatre, restaurant, or lunch counter. Using the same drinking fountains, restrooms, waiting rooms, and Laundromats as blacks, not to mention sitting next to them on public transportation, would lower whites to the level of second class citizens.I had a friend years ago who was traveling in the South for the first time, and he went in to use a Laundromat and saw all the No Colored signs. He actually went up and asked someone where the machines were for colored clothing!

A good friend of mine grew up in the South and said that the only time he felt safe growing up there was on Sunday mornings, when all the KKK'ers were in church! They used religion and the churches to transfer blame and guilt to make the victims look like the criminals and the real criminals the victims, and it helped remove guilt from them.

The atrocities committed against people in slavery were extreme, and the chain of psychological destruction is still with us today. The destruction of the family was probably the most harmful, and once instituted is hard to reverse, so it will take *extreme changes* in society and our public school programs to make positive changes.

During the time of slavery people were property that could be sold for monetary gain, so frequently people were bred like animals and the children that were produced seldom knew who their fathers were. This is one of the things that helped produce the matriarchal black families that we see so often nowadays.

After having so many experiences in Africa there are times when I believe that African Americans should wear signs reading "Made In America", as being in an interracial family I seem to be involved with these problems on a daily basis. So far I have not seen any of the social advantages that we often hear so much about.

I believe that our military-industrial complex is probably the most destructive force for education

Even though I had a good experience in the military—because there was no war at that time, and I had a good job—when I was teaching, I began to realize the negative effects on children and learning caused by the military-industrial complex. Many of the students in the San Diego area came from military families, and I began to realize what an enormously destructive force this is and has been in our history, and what negative effects it has on learning. Parents being away from their families is bad enough, but being exposed to neurotoxins and having brain trauma or limbs blown off, not to mention the psychological destruction of killing and watching comrades being killed, are just a few of the experiences that cause military parents to pass on negative problems to their children.

There probably is no more destructive force in the United States than our own military-industrial complex. It is hard to know where to begin. It isn't just the military that causes the problems … but the *wars that do the most damage to learning!*

Brainwashing starts in the military with thinking that killing is normal, which of course is not true, and this in itself causes some psychological problems. Military people frequently bring these problems home with them and cause them to treat their children in negative ways, and this has a negative effect on the family and the ability of their children to learn.

Military people are required to move often, and changing schools is disruptive for children and their education. Frequently, the parent is missing from the child's life temporarily, if not permanently. The parent returns from war with permanent psychological problems that not only affect the child but the whole family. Killing and watching others being killed, especially if they are your buddies and innocent people, will cause emotional pain that can't help but be passed on to the family, causing learning problems.

Entire books could and probably have been written about the destructiveness of the military and war, but I am beginning to believe that our military-industrial complex is doing more damage to us than it is saving us from.

Indiscriminate use of chemicals by the military

For a long time, chemicals have been used in warfare, but one that was used on our own was nicotine. The tobacco industry provided cigarettes for years in the rations that our military received, knowing that they were addictive, and that once they had you, it was usually for life, probably a shortened one. Men came home from the military and filled their children's lives with secondhand smoke, which we know now to be detrimental to learning.

The military uses chemicals that will be destructive for many years to come, and again, books are written on this subject. Agent Orange is still causing problems with veterans from Vietnam, and Vietnam still has not been able to clean up the mess, which is affecting their entire population in adverse ways. In our recent wars, the military is using radioactive munitions that will be affecting the military personnel as well as the countries they are fighting in for many years to come, eventually causing children to have learning problems in many countries as well as the United States.

Posttraumatic stress disorder and depleted uranium

One in five veterans returning from Iraq reported a mental health problem, and one in four suffers from posttraumatic stress disorder. Combat exposure is an important contributing factor. Nearly two million service members have been deployed to Iraq and Afghanistan, and many problems include domestic violence, homicide, substance abuse, posttraumatic stress disorder (PTSD), homelessness, marital difficulties, and the ultimate—suicide. Living with a parent with any of these problems is likely to cause learning problems for their children.

PTSD has become epidemic among military personnel returning from service, and while the disorder is depicted as purely psychosomatic, it may not be just that. Since the Gulf War, and from the Balkans to the Middle East and Afghanistan, the military has used *depleted uranium.*

Some are beginning to think that depleted uranium, because of its association with the large numbers of people with posttraumatic stress disorder, may be the culprit. There are increasing rates of mutation, medical problems, and cancer in the troops who have fought in Iraq and Afghanistan and the population who live where nuclear waste is being used by the military. The incidence of suicide is even higher by people who are exposed to this chemical. Depleted uranium is used by the military because it does more damage to the objects that it is used on, with little regard for the people that encounter this potentially lethal product that has a toxic life of many years.

The United States was well aware of the potential effects on civilians and military personnel of the chemical toxicity and radiological properties of DU ammunition long before the Gulf War, and this has been stated in government documents.

Birth defects and learning problems are extreme in Iraq, where 315 tons of depleted uranium was left, and there seems to be little doubt that this is the culprit.

Agent Orange

There is evidence that *Agent Orange,* used in large quantities in Vietnam, has caused neurological problems there, and an effort is being made to clean it up. Veterans here in the States have also had serious problems, from skin lesions to cancer, and it has become obvious that these physical problems were caused by coming into contact with this chemical. There is also the great likelihood that many problems have been passed on to their children. Psychological and neurological problems are not quite so easy to associate with contact to chemicals, but when the health problems associate themselves repeatedly with the chemical, it becomes obvious that there is a causal effect.

People are coming home from these wars not only with psychological problems that are likely to affect their children's learning, but when they come home and commit suicide, there is no doubt that the child's learning will be affected at school. It is also common for children having problems to be disruptive, which is hard on the teachers and has an adverse effect on the learning of other students in the class.

Gulf War Syndrome

Nerve agents, pesticides, and anti-nerve gas drugs may be causing chronic fatigue, severe muscle pain, memory loss, and other illnesses in about 250,000 Persian Gulf War veterans. Children living with parents having these problems are likely to have learning problems.

President Eisenhower warned us about the problems with the military-industrial complex. This dichotomy is especially insidious because it is half socialist, the military, and half capitalist, the industrial complex. The industrial part can manipulate the socialist part to gain wealth. In order to assure income, there is even the possibility that military problems are actually created in order to justify the need for our enormous militarily-industrial complex. It is quite hard to justify any of the wars since World War II.

Capitalists don't like paying for the cleanup of the military, industrial pollution, and the medical and psychological costs attributed to war, but to keep the whole system going, they must pay, and it may eventually bankrupt the nation. These expenses never seem to be budgeted into the cost of a war!

In any event, wars and the problems they create will have to be paid for, for many years to come. The military is the socialist part of the military-industrial complex, and the industrial part is the capitalistic part, which makes money off the military part! The industrial half uses the military (socialist government part) to extort money out of the government.

I believe that I have given some good reasons why I consider the military-industrial complex the greatest contributor to *why children don't learn* in our society today.

The military is great for taking property back, such as taking Europe back after German's invasion or the South Pacific after Japan's takeover, but how do you fight an ideology or religion with the military? What does the enemy look like? What color is their uniform? How do you identify the enemy? Why are we in their country? What is the true objective of the fighting?

One of the real causes of 9/11 was that the Saudis wanted our military base out of their country because it was offensive to them. We took the base out, but the military still needed a reason to exist, so we went after a known tyrant. Please explain to me how we destroyed the infrastructure of an entire country and killed hundreds of thousands of their people, and many of our own, just going after one man.

Another aspect of this is that we have military bases in about 130 to 140 different countries in the world. Do we ever think about what we would do if a foreign country came here and built a base, even with our government's approval? I'm sure we would all become terrorists!

Too often, our government and our military keep foreign leaders in power when the people of the country would like to get rid of a bad regime.

The enormous damage done to human beings by wars has been recognized for a long time. I have almost fifty letters written by my great-grandfather while fighting in the Civil War. The first one was dated March 15, 1861, from Lexington, Kentucky, and was written to a childhood girlfriend, asking if it would be okay for him to write to her. He wanted to know if she was married ... or if she'd just as soon not be bothered with his letters.

The return letter from her, dated March 22, 1863, from Columbus, Ohio, let him know that she would like to communicate with him, but the letter states, "As a general thing[,] a rather worthless set of young men return. So many are ruined by joining the army, yet they need not be, although they are surrounded by many temptations—if they only remember and follow the good advice they received before leaving home and are continually receiving in letters from home." They continued to exchange letters, and after the war was over, they were married. Their first child was my grandmother.

My younger sister Janet is a much better writer than I am, and she is writing a book based on these letters and that time in our family.

At this time the need for a large number of sophisticated arms is probably less necessary than any time in our history. This is because in the past countries were completely independent but now they are all so interdependent that to have a traditional war with another country would be like the left hand cutting off the right hand. An example of this is where China carries much of our debt and supplies us with so many things that it would be ludicrous for them to attack us. I believe that a large military force is good because it would be a deterrent and excellent for other emergencies like hurricanes and earthquakes to help with relief, but the need for a war is near zero. We should definitely think seriously before spending scarce money on fancy weaponry.

Capitalists' need for cheap labor today is negatively affecting families, children, and learning

As I travel down the different nearby avenues and go through shopping malls, I realize that in every business, almost all the employees are earning minimum wages. In the San Diego area, one cannot rent a place with earnings from a minimum wage job. Where do these people get the money for food, clothing, transportation, health care, retirement, and the many other expenses encountered by a family? It usually means that all members of a family have to work, and each one may work more than one job, and this means no time for family, the children, and their education.

Another problem with this is that when more than one person has to work to provide for a family, at least one person will have to drive (in Southern California) a long distance. It does not happen often that all the working people in a family can get jobs near home.

Something must be done to spread the wealth around so that everyone has enough to live on. A quick summary of the minimum it costs just for one person to live:

Food	$400 per month
Clothing	$ 50 per month
Utilities	$300 per month
Transportation	$500 per month
(Southern California, with incomplete public transportation)	
Rent	$900 per month
Retirement Savings	$300 per month
Health-care insurance	$300 per month
Entertainment	$ 30 per month (TV, movies, etc.)
Total	$2780 per month

Minimum wage ($7.25/hour) $1276 per month

Difference $1504 per month

This means that a parent earning minimum wage must work two jobs to support a family, or at least two people must be working and at least one parent would probably have to commute a long distance, which adds to pollution and the time the parents can spend with their children. Children in such families are less likely to have parental attention, supervision, and control, and because of the stress of this kind of living, they are more likely to suffer neglect and abuse. Neglect and abuse of a child at an early age is likely to start the "neurotic chain," which causes learning problems. The "slaves" are still not being paid enough for their contributions to society, but the masters are making more than ever!

In my own neighborhood sometimes there are more than one family living in one apartment because families have such low incomes and sometimes even to the point that they rotate sleeping in the same bed.

People making minimum wage cannot afford to own and drive a car, and unlike during the Great Depression, we don't have cheap electric transportation to get to work, so we have a real dilemma. In Southern California, workers usually have to drive long distances to work, and our public transportation systems are not good, so how do low-income people get to work?

The first thing we learn as children when studying Christianity is that Christ was a socialist, and Judas was the capitalist. It seems strange to me that the most antisocialist people are the ones who profess to be such devout Christians! The word socialism should not be a dirty word like the radio talk show people try to make it. There is a place for regulated socialism and a place for regulated capitalism.

Capitalism's promoters have brainwashed us into thinking that anything that makes money has to be good! This promotes an "every man for himself" philosophy that does not promote good planning for the good of everyone in the nation. If people are not paid enough to afford automobiles and there is no money to be made in public transportation, again, how do low-income people get to work? I am not against capitalism, but I think it needs regulation and controls that fit into an overall plan that meets the needs of people, society, and the nation. Too often, capitalism creates problems that it does not intend to solve, such as the mountains of trash that communities are forced to deal with, or what to do with atomic waste, and the list could go on forever.

Another fallacy of capitalism is that the people at the top with the most money are the ones that earned it! Just as the slaves "earned" it in the past, so is it happening today.

The Waltons of Walmart store fame are known to be worth over a hundred billion dollars and are one of the wealthiest families in the world. The system would have us believe that they earned the money so they should be able to keep it. They did *not* earn it! Adults and children in China working for slave-labor wages are the ones who earned it. Children in China work to help their parents out financially and are not able to attend school. These people earned the money, not the Waltons.

The other people who earned it are the people who work in the Walmart stores, working for minimum or near minimum wages that they cannot live on, so they frequently have to work more than one job. These workers don't have time for their children, and they frequently have almost no benefits, such as health care, paid vacations, or retirement programs.

Would it not make more sense to use some of the unearned billions that the Waltons have accumulated, and truly did not earn, to pay the people who actually earned the money a decent wage? They also could do a better job of providing benefits like health care and pensions which would make workers and their families more secure. Paid vacation benefits might allow them to spend more time with their families.

I was alive during the Great Depression, and the thing that ended it was when WWII started, for it gave the government permission to raise taxes, which they did, up into the 94 percent bracket for the wealthiest tax bracket. This money put everyone to work at decent salaries, the war was nearly paid for, and the wealthy were still wealthy at the war's end. Perhaps if the Waltons had known that they would have to pay 94 percent income tax, they would have paid their employees more—in other words, put the money back into their business so they wouldn't have to pay taxes on that money. It is a fallacy that business owners pay taxes on money they put back into their businesses, but many talk show hosts would like you to think that. The Waltons would still have billions even it they paid 94 percent income tax.

Nowadays, we are told that all we have to do is lower taxes on the wealthy and they will put everyone to work. Examples of Presidents Ronald Reagan, George Bush, and the second George Bush are used as times when taxes were lowered on the wealthy and they employed more people and more taxes were collected from the newly employed. There were other factors involved that usually are not mentioned when talking about this subject.

What they fail to acknowledge is that in each of those presidencies, at the same time they were lowering taxes on the wealthy, they were increasing spending on the military-industrial complex enormously, with the arms race during the Reagan administration, which caused the USSR to go bankrupt before us. Then, during the term of the first George Bush, there was the Gulf War, with enormous amounts of money spent on the military-industrial complex; and with the second Bush, two wars started after the tax cuts. The money for the wars made it look as if the tax cuts caused an upturn in income for the government.

The money put into the military-industrial complex went into salaries and back to the wealthy, who always make money on war profiteering that raised revenues and the employment statistics. Lowering taxes on the wealthy had nothing to do with a better economy and more revenue to the government during these administrations!

Even the labor tyrant Henry Ford knew that you had to pay your workers enough to afford to buy your product. Parents who are working several jobs just to make ends meet do not have time for their children and time to help them learn.

While capitalism suffers from a lack of organization, socialism seems to suffer from too much. Dictators like socialism because it lends itself to control, and the world has many examples of this in recent history.

My conclusion is that capitalism is best for some things, and socialism is best for others, and they both need good regulations. The military, much of transportation, health care, and education are logical examples of where socialism best serves the masses.

I believe that capitalism has gone past profit in the military and medical fields and is now profiteering!

Other social problems that influence learning

There was a time when everyone could be completely independent, as when the Constitution was written, but that is no longer possible. There are simply too many people and not enough land and natural resources for this to be practical. Health care and transportation were not considered problems at the time the Constitution was written, but populations, urban sprawl, transportation, and health care are problems that have become important in our lives and now need solutions for our national good.

Divorce, marriage, and the family cause learning problems

Approximately half of marriages end in divorce, and there probably had been a dysfunctional family for years before the divorce, with the negative effect on the children and learning taking place for a while. Along with the tension in the family, there may also have been verbal or psychological abuse—or even more traumatic experiences. The emotions caused by the actual breakup of the family are extremely traumatic, with many complications that are likely to affect learning.

There may be new stepparents and the mixture of families, with new brothers and sisters. As family dynamics change, there are bound to be emotional problems.

The child may be left with only one parent trying to provide for the whole family and with financial problems that will add to the stress. There probably were emotional problems by one or both parents that may have included self-medication (drugs), which could have been a factor in causing the divorce. Self-medication just complicates problems and makes everything worse, and all of the above is bound to have a negative effect on a child and his learning abilities.

For about ten years, I worked between two schools, and my office was in the career center of both schools, but in the second school two coaches also had offices. We usually had athletes as our office assistants, as this would assure that they kept their grades up. One year we had a black football player as one of our assistants, and he was bright and helpful. One day the subject of family and divorce came up, and he said that he was living with both birth parents, and I said that was great, as not many students now have that luxury. The last day of school, I mentioned how lucky he was to be living with both birth parents. He looked at me and said that his father was a drug addict who abused him and his mother regularly. Even when it seems that children are in good functioning families, that's not always the case, and this may explain why this student had some learning problems.

TV, computers, electronic games, cell phones, etc., cause learning problems

The average person spends over four hours a day watching television, and this is time that parents could be spending with their children, doing positive bonding and helping children with their studies.

Children who watch too much TV may be more bonded to the television than they are with their parents, and schoolwork will surely be affected. Adding to the negative effect of too much TV is that much of the programming is not that wholesome, and there is the probability of it having a negative effect on the child.

I generally consider computers mostly positive, but when children use computer games as their "drug of choice," they probably are spending too much time playing on them, which is probably a symptom of other problems that are going to affect learning.

I have noticed that children with ADD or ADHD not only find relief from their problems with computer games, but this is an area where they can excel, so it may help build self-esteem, which is a positive thing. However, all the electronic devices nowadays mostly keep children from many of the educational things they should be doing—and keep their parents from spending time with them.

In many cases, the use of these devices is a symptom of neurosis! Frequently, the neurosis has been caused by capitalists, and the capitalists are making money off the devices.

Conception, abortion, birth control, and adoption cause learning problems

Logical thinking should take place when it comes to when life begins, and the fallacy is that life begins at conception. The illustration below shows that this is not the case.

If you have fried eggs for breakfast, and then someone later asks what you ate for breakfast, do you say that you ate fried chicken? No, but there is a time when there is a chicken forming in the egg and you would not eat it, and there is a time when logically it is too late to do an abortion. It never is a good thing, but done as early as possible is in most cases better than bringing another unwanted child into this world. (One of the reasons eggs used to be candled was to make sure a chicken was not forming in the egg.)

To say that life begins at conception and that a baby is being killed at this time is an emotional judgment and does not show good logic.

How in the world can conception, abortion, birth control, and adoption cause learning problems? They all have to do with bringing another unwanted child into this world and an unwanted child is much more likely to have learning disabilities than a wanted child. With five hundred thousand "throwaway children" in foster care, our nation doesn't need more children that likely will not only have many social problems but learning problems as well.

No one is in favor of abortion!

I am tired of people inferring that because people are not in favor of outlawing abortion, that that means they are in favor of it. We need to be realistic.

When I was young, abortion was against the law, and that did not stop it any more than Prohibition stopped people from drinking alcohol. People just made their own alcohol and consumed it illegally.

When abortion was illegal, women did their own, resulting in many deaths from improper methods and unsterile conditions. When abortion is not legal, there is no counseling available for women on this subject and it is much more likely that they will try to do this themselves as was the case when abortion was illegal.

Logically, we can only hope to lower the abortion rate, not eliminate it, and it would be much better to use birth control instead of abortion. We must provide knowledge about birth control to all people. *Abortion is the worst form of birth control!*

The better methods of birth control available now should be used instead of abortion. Abortion should take place only early in the pregnancy, when there are only a few cells that can only be seen under a microscope, and it should only be performed after proper counseling. Much more should be done to assure that things don't even get to the abortion stage.

If abortion becomes illegal, will we put women in jail for performing their own? Will we give all women of childrearing age pregnancy tests monthly, and if they are pregnant one month and not the next, will we arrest them for murder and try them in court? The whole subject needs to be looked at much more realistically and with some logic. If this subject was not so emotionally and politically charged, public thinking on this subject would probably be much closer than we might think. We need to stop using it as a "cause" for politicians and religious fanatics. We all want the same thing, and that is to limit abortions as much as possible; we just have to realize that it would be impossible to eliminate them completely.

I did not find out until my mother was deteriorating from age and I had to take over her corespondence that she had changed from a Republican to a Democrat. When I asked her about this, she told me that when she entered the nursing profession in the early 1930s, many of her patients had been women who had tried to perform their own abortions and had botched the procedure. Many of them died.

If abortion is against the law, women can't even get proper care or counseling in this area. The people who are so much in favor of outlawing abortion should be required to start adopting some of the five hundred thousand children already in foster care. Perhaps we should start with Rush Limbaugh and Ann Coulter taking in a dozen or two each. Oh, I forgot that most people who criticize Planned Parenthood and abortion don't even want to be taxed to take care of these children let alone take some of these children in and adopt them!

At any given time in this nation, there are approximately half a million throwaway children in the adoption and foster care systems, children whose mothers either could not support them or did not want them. Unwanted children are much more likely to have learning problems, because their parents more than likely had problems that led to the need to give the child up for adoption.

Homeless people may have children, and these children are likely to have learning problems

Homeless people are symptoms of other societal problems. They are often mentally ill, and frequently they are veterans that have been made that way by the horrors of war. Killing and watching others die and be torn apart is just not normal. If children are living with parents who have serious problems, these problems are likely to have a negative effect on the children and their learning.

In recent years, politicians have closed our mental hospitals and other facilities where the mentally ill could get help, and these facilities were not replaced with anything better. Ronald Reagan was responsible for this in California.

Now most people with emotional or psychological problems are homeless, in prison, or in foster care or orphanages, where they not only are not getting the treatment they need, but they don't have a sense of belonging anywhere. All too often, these people are mistreated and traumatized, which is more of what probably got them in the situation to begin with.

Homelessness is the result of a more serious social problem that eventually must be addressed.

People in prison may have children, and these children are likely to have learning problems

Another symptom of a problem is that some 283,800 inmates are identified as having a mental illness. This represents 16 percent of the inmate populations of state and local jails. Jails have effectively become America's new mental institutions; they house a larger volume of mentally ill people than all other programs combined. However, these inmates rarely receive the treatment that they need and have a right to. The criminal justice system is overpopulated and under-equipped to deal with psychotic disorders requiring mental health care services.

Prisons just make mentally ill people even worse because they are misunderstood and frequently mistreated. It is even likely that the mental illness was caused by mistreatment, abuse, and trauma at an early age.

Privatizing or making money off other people's mental health problems is disgusting to me. I read one statistic that estimates that 60 percent of the people in prison have ADD or ADHD.

People in prison are often parents of children who are having learning problems in our public school systems. Children with parents in prison not only do not have that person in their lives, but they have to contend with the stigma of having a parent in prison. We might say that the child is better off without this "bad" parent, but that doesn't make the learning problems go away, and just the fact that the child has a parent in prison may cause the student to become the object of intolerance.

The United States has the highest documented incarceration rate in the world. It is approximately 754 inmates per one hundred thousand people, *a rate nearly five times the world average*! About one in every thirty-one adults in this country is in jail or on supervised release. Are we the most evil people in the world ... or *are we doing something wrong*?

The needs of capitalism may be the cause of many people going to jail, and this same need may be what is causing learning problems.

On average, it costs $55.09 per day to keep a person in prison, or about $20,108 per year for each detainee. It also cost society more to educate children with learning problems.

Legal drugs and illegal drugs all make money for capitalists

Prescription drugs are now being given to more than half a million children and adolescents in America for psychological problems, and many of these problems may have been caused by by-products of the chemical industry that come into contact with parents and children. A Columbia University study recently found a doubling of the rate of prescribing antipsychotic drugs for two- to five-year-olds from 2000 to 2007. They often say that these children could not attend school without the drugs, but even with these drugs, these children have learning problems.

Self-medication is usually the symptom of a problem, and the person usually is not prescribing the right medication in the right dosage. The medication adds to the problem and then creates a sociological problem which we are not doing a good job of dealing with at this time. Too often, the medication just adds another factor in an already bad situation.

I feel that children and parents that self-medicate to ease emotional and psychological pain just complicate learning problems. Often the parents are so consumed with their own problems and easing their own pain that children are not receiving the love and attention they need, and there may be abuse and other traumatic experiences as well. Whether the drug use is by relatives, friends, or by the child, the child's learning abilities are likely to be diminished.

The child frequently has *no sense of belonging*, may have learning disabilities from the drug use of the parents, and the list could go on and on. Society has a problem that is affecting not only society but our schools as well, and we cannot expect the schools to come up with solutions to psychological problems and the learning disabilities that they are being presented with.

At this time, Mexico, our neighbor to the south, is having enormous problems with drug cartels killing law enforcement people and other cartel people trying to supply the great demand for drugs in the United States. The same things that are causing learning problems for children may be what are causing their parents and frequently the students to self-medicate. It is time that we began to treat the real problem and not just the symptoms, which have also become problems. I am convinced that most emotional problems start in early childhood—from neglect, no feeling of belonging, abuse (both physical and verbal), and generally the lack of a loving family. Self-medication is the symptom of a problem and just adds another problem to the person's life.

Secondhand smoke causes learning problems for all, but especially for African American children

African American children are the most exposed to secondhand smoke of any children in the United States. Mothers who smoke are more likely to have children with a high risk of "conduct disorder." This psychiatric disorder in children produces higher juvenile delinquency rates, frequent and persistent lying, vandalism, sexual aggressiveness, and stealing. Along with these problems will come learning problems in school.

Approximately 26 percent of children less than five years old live in homes with at least one adult smoker. Illnesses requiring hospitalization are as high as fifteen thousand! From secondhand smoke alone, impairment in school performance and intellectual achievement has been demonstrated.

Third-hand smoke has been studied at San Diego State University

This is the tobacco smoke contamination that is left behind after people have smoked in a building. One would think that this would not be harmful, but scientific studies have shown that even after rooms have been cleaned, small children have nicotine in their urine after living in these rooms. While this may not have a negative effect on adults, it may cause lower IQ in a child's developing brain.

Teachers have known for a long time that sugar causes problems in the classroom

Because of its concentration, *sugar* is one of the items that should be considered a drug. The enormous amount of sugar consumed in the United States is causing one of the highest rates of diabetes and destruction of all body parts and health in general, which should be cause for alarm.

I learned over fifty years ago after I was in the auto accident and had some problems with arthritis that I had to curtail my intake of sugar to control pain.

Teachers have long felt that sugar plays a negative roll in discipline and learning; and many mental health professionals refer to sugar as the love substitute for neurotics.

Religion can be a capitalistic organization and cause learning problems

We have some religious leaders trying to tell us that our country was founded on Christian principles. I would therefore like to ask this question: Why would Christians install unregulated capitalism as their economic system when it is contrary to Christ's teachings? Again, Christ was a socialist; Judas was the capitalist.

The foundation of capitalism in this country was slavery, and when capitalism is not controlled, the system seems to revert to its foundation. Capitalists have a neurotic need for cheap labor and for the accumulation of wealth, control, and dominance over people; capitalism is the vehicle they use to get their psychological "fix."

If this nation was founded on Christian principles, where were these principles when the greatest genocide in the history of the world was perpetrated against the American Indian? Capitalists gained large amounts of land with lots of cheap raw materials but left a defeated people with problems that still need to be dealt with. As usual, socialism is expected to clean up the mess that capitalists made.

Where were these principles when people from Africa were enslaved, working for nothing and having their families destroyed in many ways, such as selling their children to make even more money? The remnants of this destruction are still felt to this day and causing learning problems that affect us as a nation.

Where were these principles when people were being lynched? Where were they when all the Jim Crow laws were enacted?

Why didn't these principles keep such a destructive war from taking place in order to end slavery? Slavery took place along the east coast of South America, in Central America, on the east coast of North America, and throughout all of the Caribbean, and in every other place, slavery ended without a major war.

I think Christ would be disappointed in the way his principles have been misused!

I look at many organized religions as big business and their schools as a means of supplying their clientele for this business. Organized religion is usually careful in keeping their financial business confidential. This is the reason government should not support private schools any more than they would support any other private business. For me, organized religion detracts from spirituality because it turns the whole matter into a moneymaking business.

Some religious groups hope to build clientele by inflicting their prayers on public schoolchildren in the hope that this will win them over to their beliefs. This would have a disastrous effect, as they would want denominational prayers that would cause intolerance. There was a time when all students came from similar religious beliefs, but now there is such a diverse cultural mix in our public schools that allowing one group special privileges of denominational prayer would cause disruption on school campuses. I'm sure that I said silent prayers every day in the pubic schools as I taught, and no one stopped me!

A better way to promote spirituality might be to provide a quiet meditation room, devoid of religious decoration, where all children and even teachers could go to pray or meditate. Even atheists might feel welcome in a place like this, and it would provide a place where Muslim students could put their prayer rugs down and pray.

I don't think there was a day in the thirty-five years that I taught that I did not pray, but I did not force my prayer on any one else.

Separation of church and state is not specific in the US Constitution, but we have pretty much lived by this doctrine throughout the history of the country. It is what has let us live together in harmony, with many different denominations living together, much better than in most places of the world. We not only are diverse religiously but also racially, ethnically, and insofar as place of origin and sexual orientation. Separation of church and state is truly the only area in which I am at odds with the Muslim religion, as they believe the church should be the ruler, and that makes it rather incompatible with other beliefs.

Whenever a group is looked down upon or a person is perceived to be inferior, it can create disruptions in the learning process. Students who were victims of intolerance in the school setting committed some of the recent school shootings. For this reason, schools try to promote tolerance and acceptance of all lifestyles, and they are frequently criticized for seeming to promote or be partial to people who are perceived to be inferior. Within the public school systems, tolerance is an important factor in the harmonious functioning of the school. Private schools can just get rid of the problems and be as intolerant as they wish to be.

Chapter 22

Capitalism's Needs May Also Cause Inherited Disorders That May Be Causing Learning Problems

The following conditions are usually thought of as inherited, but are they inherited because their parents were exposed to environmental waste chemicals that may have affected DNA or genes during the reproductive process? There is much we don't know, but because of the chemicals that our society encounters, we can bet that good things are not happening.

IQ

There are enormous differences in students, and an average teacher may get students with high IQs and no students with discipline problems in their classes, while a good teacher may get students with low IQs and learning problems. The hardworking teacher would not look as good as the average teacher with high-performing students.

We would like to think that we are all created equal, but when it comes to intelligence, we are only equal in the eyes of God, for there can be a wide range in individual IQs. A child's intelligence will affect his or her capacity for learning.

All teachers learn about the IQ bell curve. This is a specialized graph that shows how people's capacity for learning is spread out, with those few having a low capacity for learning at the left side of the bell, and a few at the right side having a high capacity to learn—often with near photographic memories and a great capacity to process and use information. The majority of people are in the center, where the curve goes way up, but half of the people are below average and half are above. The bell curve is assigned two hundred points, so the average would be in the center, at one hundred points, and that is where most people are located on the graph.

IQ (intelligence quotient) is a number meant to measure people's cognitive abilities (intelligence) in relation to their age group. An IQ between 90 and 110 is considered average, and over 120 is believed to be superior.

Roughly 68 percent of the population has an IQ between 85 and 115. About 95 percent of the population scores between 70 and 130. A score below 70 may indicate mental retardation, and a score above 130 may indicate intellectual giftedness. About 1 percent of the population has an IQ of 136 or higher. However, an individual scoring 100 within one population can score above or below that value within another population. For example, the Japanese are supposed to have the highest average IQ in the world (115), but this could only be an average of 100 within their own population of Japan.

IQ tests are intended to measure a person's ability to absorb and repeat mechanical intellectual tasks, and since the IQ is described as a "quotient," it usually represents the ratio between a person's "mental age" and actual chronological age. IQ is considered to be inherited, which means that significant variation in IQ between adults can be attributed to genetic variation, and the environment plays a role.

The history of the IQ started with the Binet-Simon scale in 1905, with one single goal in mind: to serve as a guide to identify children in school who need special education or extra help to minimize their inferior levels. Binet also reported that it's not designed to measure "intelligence." Later, after many modifications on the original method of Binet-Simon, the Stanford-Binet test was born, and then refined testing methods were developed. Today intelligence tests are becoming more popular among the population as well as in government departments. In 1989, the American Academy for the Advancement of Science listed the IQ test among the twenty most significant scientific discoveries of the twentieth century, along with nuclear fission, DNA, and flight.

I am not a specialist in IQs, but I have a hard time believing that those with less than a 100 IQ can make it through college, and often we waste time and money trying to convince everyone that they can.

Since I started writing this, there is scientific evidence that chemicals in the environment can cause a child's IQ to go down many points. Studies are showing that secondhand smoke is even lowering IQs in children who are exposed, and this is especially true of African American children. Also, scientists have discovered a relationship between pesticides on fruits and vegetables and ADD and ADHD!

ADD and ADHD

Attention deficit disorder is a biologically-based condition. The neurological condition causes a persistent pattern of difficulties, resulting in one or more of the following behaviors: inattention, impulsivity, hyperactivity.

These are some of the most common symptoms. People with ADD have difficulty attending to or focusing on a specific task, and they may become distracted within a matter of minutes. Inattentive behavior may also cause difficulties with staying organized (e.g., losing things), keeping track of time, completing tasks, and making careless errors.

ADHD is a difficulty inhibiting behavior, and these people are in constant motion. They may engage in excessive fiddling, leg swinging, and squirming in their chairs.

Along with the above problems, some are impulsive to the point where the person has difficulty actually controlling impulses. These people do not stop and think before they act, and they may say and do whatever comes into their minds, without thinking about the consequences. They might say something inappropriate and regret it later, blurt out a response to a question before a person is done speaking to them, or they may have difficulty waiting for their turn in line. Quite often people with ADD or

ADHD have serious problems with relationships and need help in dealing with them.

Dealing with the problems of the ADD and the ADHD students is usually outside the scope of a regular classroom, for these students can be disruptive and have other problems that would distract a teacher from the other students.

Children with the above problems know something is wrong, as their brains just go too fast. Dyslexia, depression, eating disorders, and digestive problems may also be present. Relationships are usually difficult, which means they frequently do not have the support of family and friends. They often have no sense of belonging—but they don't know how and why.

People with ADD and ADHD have such a hard time in society and relationships that they frequently end up self-medicating or in prison, or both. They usually seem to be very bright but fail at many things, and failure after failure snowballs until they start self-medicating to get relief from the emotional pain.

Most of the children I have seen with the above problems have been abused in early life, which is a failure of the family and society, and prison just adds more abuse and failure to a tormented life. Using prisons to treat emotional and psychological problems is counterproductive in our society.

Autism

This is a description of autism by the Autism Speaks organization: "Autism is a complex neurobiological disorder that typically lasts throughout a person's lifetime. It is part of a group of disorders known as autism spectrum disorders (ASD). Today, 1 in 110 individuals is diagnosed with autism. It occurs in all racial, ethnic, and social groups, and it is four times more likely to strike boys than girls. Autism impairs a person's ability to communicate and relate to others. It is also associated with rigid routines and repetitive behaviors, such as obsessively arranging objects or following specific routines. Symptoms can range from mild to quite severe."

Dealing with a neurological disorder of this magnitude is also beyond the scope of the classroom teacher. The teacher would need to spend all of his or her time with this student, and it still wouldn't be effective. Special people trained in this specific neurological disorder should be working with these children. Is there the possibility that autism is caused by altered DNA from foreign chemicals?

Dyslexia

Dyslexia is a neurologically based, often inherited, disorder that interferes with the acquisition and processing of language. It is different in each person, but it is manifested by difficulties in receptive and expressive language, which includes the processing of reading, writing, spelling, and handwriting. It is well recognized that boys have problems or are just slower developing is this area, and it seems to me that the part of the brain that processes reading just develops later in some boys.

Dyslexia is not the result of lack of motivation, sensory impairment, inadequate instructional or environmental opportunities, or other limiting conditions, but it may occur together with these conditions.

One thing that might help in dealing with dyslexia it to have all textbook publishers provide video and audio transcripts of their books so at least these students can be presented with the information rather than just staring at books that they have no possibility of reading. In many cases materials used for dyslexia would also be appropriate for blind students.

Although dyslexia is lifelong, individuals with dyslexia frequently respond successfully to timely and appropriate intervention, and that part of the brain that processes reading may at times just be late maturing. In later years, people who had problems when they were young are sometimes able to overcome them.

Hormones and vaccines

The food industry fills its animals with vaccines and hormones in order to make them fatter, and then we eat the meat and wonder why we are getting fatter. Even more serious is that little girls are going through puberty at seven and eight years old, most likely because of these hormones. If these hormones are causing these changes in girls, what are they doing to boys? Will we soon have an asexual society? There is also no doubt that these effects on children are likely to influence their learning.

Summary

The examples of neurological disorders above are just some samples of problems teachers nowadays are being asked to deal with, and they are *not* problems teachers are trained to deal with. If the teachers were to try to deal with these problems, they would just be taking time away from other students and they would not be effective with the people with any of the above disorders. In most cases, these conditions are so complex that they require a team of specialists to deal with them.

Chapter 23

Education Is Like a Three-Legged Stool

E ducation should be examined like a three-legged stool: one leg, the school board and administration; another leg, the teachers, school facilities, and curriculum; and the third leg, the students. It is the student leg that I concern myself with here.

Right-wing pundits keep attention on two of these legs, the teachers and the schools, in order to avoid examining the third, the student, which is where we should be committing more attention.

In the third leg, the material the leg is made of could be likened to the inherited intelligence, and we refer to this as the IQ, which is in a bell curve, with lower intelligence on the left half—perhaps weaker but still usable—and the upright half being higher intelligence, with stronger material to hold up the stool. Some legs may be made out of weaker materials, while others are made of stronger materials.

Then perhaps a heavy person sits on the stool, cracking the leg or partially breaking it from the seat. We could liken this to neglect, abuse, and lack of attention and a sense of belonging, causing neuroticism, psychosis, and psychotic behavior.

Then say that the leg is attacked by neurotoxins, chemicals like lead, mercury, and copper, to name a few, that compromise the material that the leg is made from. The leg's integrity may also be compromised by salt, fat, hormones, and engineered substances such as sugar, vaccines, and so forth. It also has been discovered that our foods do not have the same nutrients that they did just a few years ago. All these things might be likened to not maintaining the leg of the stool as one would take care of a piece of furniture. To make this clearer, I am trying to show that our students have problems that are not the doing of the schools and the teachers—the other *two legs just cannot hold up the stool by themselves.*

The third leg has been deteriorated by hundreds of years of psychological destruction, chemical corrosion, neglect, and inherited disabilities.

A child will have approximately seven teachers from kindergarten to sixth grade, and approximately thirty teachers from seventh to twelfth grade and this number could be quite higher. It does not make sense that thirty-seven or more teachers are all bad—and that that is why the child never learned.

Students do a fair job of getting rid of bad teachers, and I have seen many tenured teachers let go, as tenure only means that an administrator has to show cause or document reasons to fire teachers. It is actually easier to work hard and be a good teacher than it is to be a bad one, because students can tell when a teacher knows their subject and is able to impart learning and have their materials organized, and they show these teachers more respect and generally will give them less trouble. Teaching is not such an easy job that you would go into it just to make money and do nothing.

Even if a teacher has just one child in a classroom with a mild learning problem, one not requiring special education, it can cause a teacher to look bad. The teacher is likely to spend more time with that student, both in trying to teach him and possibly dealing with the likelihood of discipline problems.

EDUCATION'S THREE LEG STOOL

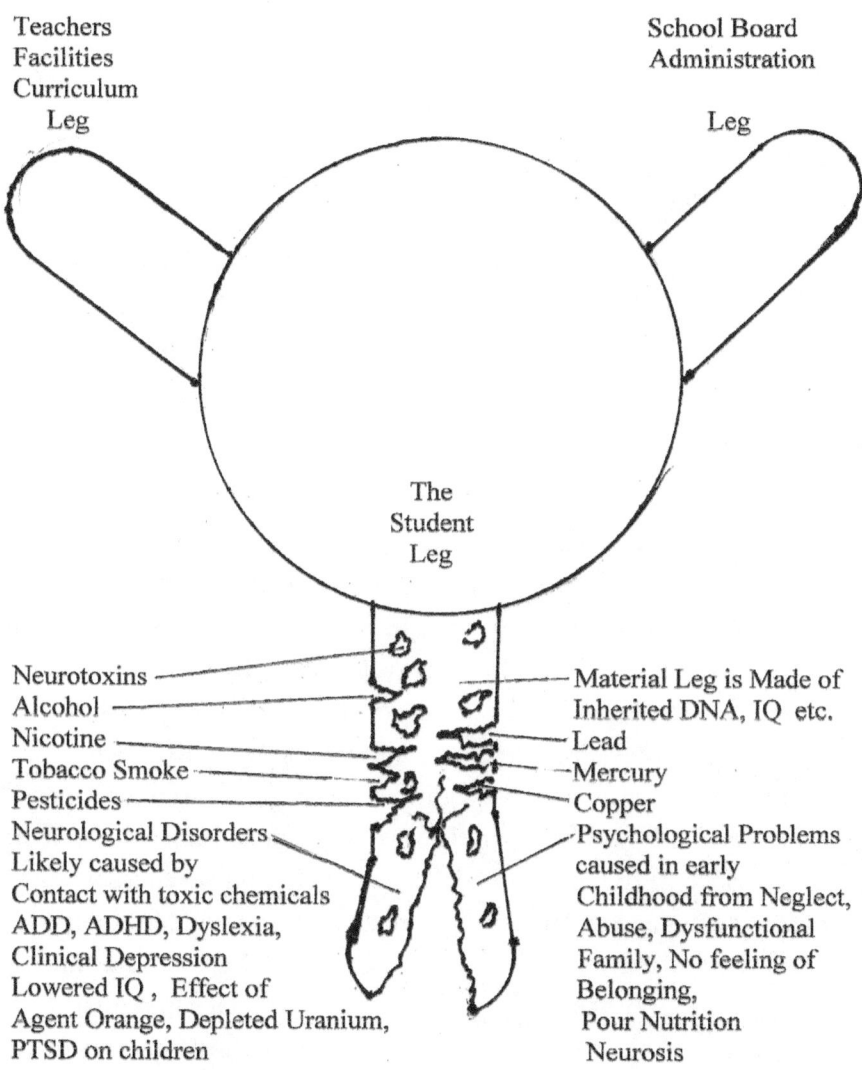

Teachers
Facilities
Curriculum
   Leg

School Board
Administration

   Leg

The
Student
Leg

Neurotoxins
Alcohol
Nicotine
Tobacco Smoke
Pesticides
Neurological Disorders
Likely caused by
Contact with toxic chemicals
ADD, ADHD, Dyslexia,
Clinical Depression
Lowered IQ , Effect of
Agent Orange, Depleted Uranium,
PTSD on children

Material Leg is Made of
Inherited DNA, IQ etc.
Lead
Mercury
Copper
Psychological Problems
caused in early
Childhood from Neglect,
Abuse, Dysfunctional
Family, No feeling of
Belonging,
Pour Nutrition
Neurosis

Education's three-legged stool

Chapter 24

Capitalists' Needs Are Protected by Highly Paid Pundits

I certainly do not pretend to be an expert in socialism or capitalism, but it does seem to me that the evils of socialism are more open and in your face, while the evils of capitalism are more difficult to attribute to capitalism, as they are frequently the waste that is in the air, water, and soil—not identifiable until after they have done their damage. Then there is the human waste—people used and abused and then discarded.

Capitalists will never admit to guilt or causing any problems, nor will they take responsibility for their criminal activity, so they employ right-wing spokespeople to protect them. These people, and we all know them, from Rush Limbaugh to Ann Coulter, make enormous amounts of money, usually associating themselves with the Christian religion and using it to help them shift criminality and guilt from the criminal capitalists.

Pundits control voters, and lobbyists control legislators, all in the interest of the capitalists and to the detriment of children and learning. The statements they frequently use are "Government is the problem" and "Get government out of our lives." This all sounds good, but I'm afraid they really mean not to let government regulate us, as this will limit our profits, even at the expense of the children of our nation.

Sometimes it actually seems as though we are regressing back to the master-slave system, and the pundits listed below, as well as many more, are the overseers, using their verbal whips to control the enslaved. They speak with authority on subjects that they are frequently not qualified to discuss, and in doing so, they are doing damage to our nation and especially our children and their learning abilities.

The right-wing pundits transfer guilt and destroy their enemies.

Capitalists' need for money causes them to destroy controls and those who try to control them, and when their pundits fail, they transfer blame to the entity that steps in to save them. What is even harder to believe is that they even try to destroy their savior! We saw this in the recent near collapse of capitalism, when President Obama intervened and probably saved the nation from the worst depression the world has ever seen. Often they use religion in their battles to protect capitalism.

Mrs. Carter made a statement referring to one of the Republican presidents that followed her husband: "He makes us feel comfortable with our prejudices." I think this would apply to almost all the right-wing pundits.

Below are just a few of the people making money protecting corporate America from being regulated and taking responsibility for the messes and problems they cause. We should always remember that money is *their* drug of choice.

It should concern us all that these rather emotionally out-of-control entities are also the ones that control the guns in our nation. If I remember correctly, Dick Cheney seems to have a hard time controlling his gun, or maybe it's his drinking and shooting …

Most of the people named below, and many others, frequently speak with authority on subjects that they are not knowledgeable about and have not earned the right to pontificate about. I would just like to take a moment to name several—and their actions that transfer attention away from problems caused by capitalism or transfer guilt from the guilty to the victims and the innocent. They also work to control the voters on behalf of capitalism, often using half-truths and lies, and it sounds good to say, "Government is the problem" or "Get government out of our business." But this is what they really mean: "Don't regulate our pollution!"

Pat Robertson

Pat Robertson tried to make Haitians the guilty ones after their earthquake, saying that God was punishing them for destroying the capitalistic system in Haiti, where the master-slave system was providing wonderful products like sugar, cotton, indigo, and other goods. They put those entire wonderful plantation owners out of business, all because they didn't enjoy being worked to death for no pay, having their families destroyed, and the list could go on and on.

Dick Cheney

Halliburton, Dick Cheney's old company, operates offshore so it does not have to pay taxes, and those taxes could go to help pay the enormous costs of taking care of the medical and psychological needs of our service personnel and their families. These problems eventually end up in the public school classrooms. Halliburton makes money war profiteering, the people have to pay for the enormous damages done, and the right-wing pundits make money transferring blame to the government and making it sound as if a socialist government caused the problem. They try to prove their talking points that less government would solve all our problems. We may have less government now, but we have more out-of-control government contractors.

Early in Dick Cheney's time in office, he spent a lot of time in secret meetings with oil executives; I am sure he was making many concessions to them so that his buddies in that industry could make more money.

The right-wing pundits spend all their time protecting capitalism by shifting responsibility and guilt, such as with the Gulf of Mexico oil spill. They tried to say that President Obama was guilty of a horrible crime because he had BP Oil Company put twenty billion dollars in an escrow fund to immediately help the people who had lost their livelihood. This was the most prudent thing to do in light of the fact that capitalism *never* cleans up its messes, and the Bhopal and Exxon Valdez situations are a good example of problems that have not been rectified in well over twenty years. The Exxon Valdez spill in the Prince William Sound occurred in 1989, and twenty-one years later, the environment has still not returned to normal, nor have the victims been properly compensated.

In 1984, in Bhopal India, the pesticide plant operated by Union Carbide, now a subsidiary of Dow Chemical Company, was cited for thirty major hazards that had not been fixed. They'd caused neurotoxins to be released, and five hundred thousand people were exposed to these chemicals. Some believe that as many as twenty thousand people may have died over the years, and the groundwater that the residents depend on is still so polluted that babies are still being born with birth defects. Twenty-five years later, 390 tons of chemicals at the plant are *still* leaking, so the environment is still being compromised, children are still being harmed, and the victims still have not been compensated. The assets of this company should have immediately been impounded until the damages were repaired and the victims compensated.

Capitalists will never voluntarily compensate their victims or clean up their messes!

George Will

George Will is one of those right-wing pundits who frequently act as an authority on public education, and until he has thirty or more years experience teaching in a variety of public schools, I wish he would quit acting as if he knows the answers. I frequently think about how all these people have never solved a problem in their lives but still make lots of money sitting on their butts and criticizing the people who are trying to solve problems. Anyone can be a critic, but solving problems is a different story.

He is a good example of a person who keeps attention on the wrong issues, putting blame for the problems in the wrong place—on the teachers and the schools. While those are important, we must also examine the student.

Sarah Palin

She is like a junior high school cheerleader with lots of right-wing emotional rhetoric and little substance. I think it would be hard for her to identify problems, prioritize them, and use a thought process such as used in plane geometry using hypotheses, axioms, postulates, theorems, and corollaries and use them in a scientific way to solve problems.

Does she live her religion or use it to make money? It seems to me that a person who believes in a loving Christ would not use guns to go out and kill his creations for sport or fun.

At the river, Uncle Bob has always put grain out for the wild deer and turkeys, and the deer will sometimes even eat out of your hands, but every once in a while, someone will come with a gun and shoot those beautiful grain-fed deer and just leave them, not even taking them for food.

Rush Limbaugh

Why does someone pay Rush thirty-three million dollars a year? Who pays this salary? What do they expect in return?

As we look at our entire structure of government and society, we need to realize that all politicians are elected into office with capitalists' money, and then they are controlled while in office by lobbyists who are paid by big business capitalists! All the information coming from radio, television, newspapers, etc., is controlled by capitalists' money. Ann Coulter would get a kick out of anyone saying she can be controlled!

To protect their interests, capitalists pay Rush Limbaugh a lot of money every year. Does anyone ever wonder why Rush is worth that much to them? Do people ever wonder how he protects their interests? If you listen to him, you will notice that any time there is an issue that might portray capitalism in a negative way, he will find a way to divert attention from the negative issue and make something or someone else the bad guy. The real criminal becomes the victim!

Being from a racially mixed family, I have always been aware that Rush was racially prejudiced, but since the election of President Obama, he has become quite overt, and it is quite obvious that he is filled with hate for the man, not just what he is trying to accomplish.

An example of this is with the health care bill. President Obama identified a serious problem and encouraged Congress to solve the problem; he himself had nothing to do with the solutions. It was obvious that the lobbyists for the insurance industry, big health-care companies and the drug companies wrote the bill, just putting in enough to make it look like something was being done. If Rush were not prejudiced, he would just concentrate on it being an imperfect bill, but he refers to it as Obama's terrible legislation. Critiquing things is healthy; destroying good leaders is bad.

It has always been obvious that he is a neurotic man, but I think he has progressed to being a psychotic person. His fifth marriage indicates that he has a serious problem with relationships, and he self-medicates to the point of addiction. But these aren't the things that concern me most.

I believe that he is as close to an Adolf Hitler as we have ever seen in this country, and he is probably very responsible for supporting the gun lobby that is producing a Gestapo-like movement in this country. He and the others have developed their hate groups just as Hitler did. These pundits have all replaced the Jews with the Mexicans and Muslims. None of these groups would be a threat if we just stopped employing Mexicans and stopped using Middle East oil. Also, it wouldn't hurt if we stopped using drugs coming from Afghanistan!

One of the things that upsets the right wing the most is that big business did not elect this president. In my lifetime, I don't believe there has been a president more elected by the people than Barack Obama, and the right wing finds him hard to control.

I am convinced that right-wing emotional hate groups should take responsibility for the assassinations of Martin Luther King Jr., Malcolm X, Robert Kennedy, and Jack Kennedy, and the same types of groups are employing racial hatred against President Obama, which could have the same results. It is sad when people feel they must use lies, half-truths, and exaggeration to whip up prejudices that are known to lie just below the surface in this country.

The pundits know that it is easy to stir up the emotional right wing, and neurotics seem to live for a cause; racism is one of the easiest to motivate. The president is trying to put reasonable controls on capitalism, and the pundits are being paid huge amounts to keep this from happening.

Michael Savage

Michael Savage admits to having a difficult childhood due to his father's "gruff and profane" personality, and he encountered frequent verbal abuse from his father. This probably accounts for his hate-filled neurosis; the hate just keeps spewing out like the toxins from the BP oil disaster in the Gulf of Mexico.

Sadly, he believes that children with autism are just undisciplined by their parents. He is a very intelligent man with a some background in teaching, and I think it would be interesting for him to teach a class with just one autistic child. I am sure he would change his mind. He might even read some of the scientific evidence concerning autism. As a teacher, he would probably just get the child transferred out of his class and not deal with the problem, but I would assure him that autism is not caused by bad parenting.

Shame on him for using the disabled instead of trying to solve the problems involved with curing autism.

I hope Michael feels the same way about businesses and industries that throw tantrums and act like spoiled brats when asked to be responsible for cleaning up their pollution and messes!

Ann Coulter

In her little hate-filled world, she uses dyslexia to describe people that she thinks cannot think for themselves, forgetting that Albert Einstein was dyslexic and was able to overcome this disability. For most people, it is a lifetime of shame and work trying to overcome this handicap, and it should never be joked about. She must have a hollow life if she has to resort to making fun of the disabled in her diatribes, but she makes lots of money at it, so I guess anything goes, no matter who she hurts. I do not know how loving people can be followers of such hate and at the same time profess to be followers of a loving Christ.

Glenn Beck

Glenn Beck tries to transfer the image of Martin Luther King Jr., who lived his religion, to himself; I see Glenn Beck as only using religion to make money and protect capitalism from being examined for its faults.

Above are examples of just a few of the people who protect capitalism, influence voters, and even subvert democracy in a way; and then there are the lobbyists that control the legislative process and subvert democracy at that level.

Another area where the lesser bad guy is made to look like the criminal is with illegal immigration from Mexico. The immigrant worker is breaking one law by coming into the country without documentation and is made to look like the worst of lawbreakers, again mostly by the right-wing media paid by capitalists.

By focusing attention on the workers, it takes attention away from the real criminals, the industries that hire them, and let's look at the laws they usually break. They usually don't pay the legal minimum wage, let alone a living wage. They may not pay Social Security taxes or the taxes on their wages. They often don't pay into workers' compensation or for health-care benefits. There is no paid vacation or retirement program. *Who is the real criminal?*

Chapter 25

Capitalist Needs Must Be Met, and Those Who Try to Regulate Will Be Destroyed

Capitalists control our government to the point that they will destroy any politician who tries to regulate or put controls on them.

President Carter

Because he dared to try to regulate capitalism, President Carter was destroyed by right-wing pundits. President Carter is an atomic physicist and a brilliant thinker, and in 1977 he proposed a brilliant energy policy for our nation. If it had been implemented, it would have put the nation in a much better place today. The reason it was not implemented is that it was an attempt to control capitalists' need for cheap energy, with all its pollution and negative effects on land, air, and water—and finally on children and learning. Because of his trying to control capitalism, its representatives, such as Rush Limbaugh, have demonized President Carter. This is a standard tactic of the right-wingers, to make the good guys look like the criminals or discredit them in any way possible.

The socialistic government steps in to try to solve problems created by capitalists, so they are there on the scene, making it easy to transfer responsibility and guilt from the guilty party, the capitalists, to the government or socialism. When the government tries to regulate capitalism, all hell breaks loose, as was the case when President Carter developed his energy policy. The right-wing nutcases not only destroyed the policy, but they are still trying to destroy the man even further. If his policies were put in place, we probably would be energy independent today, and we would not have gone through the Gulf War, the war in Iraq, and the Afghanistan mess.

President Carter also developed credit regulations to put some controls on our banking and financial systems. Most of the regulations that had been put in place after the Great Depression of the 1930s had been removed, by the right wing, so that the systems could take more chances and make more money.

President Carter is an example of a person who *lives* his religion, teaching Sunday school, helping build houses for the poor, and traveling the world trying to solve serious problems. If you are going to be a follower of people, follow the people who live their religion, not the ones who use it to make money. I have right-wing friends and relatives who are conservative Christians but are passionate followers of the right-wing hate-mongers. Lending support to such a hateful movement does not seem to be consistent with the values of a loving Christ.

President Obama
President Obama scares the right mostly because he is one of the first presidents in a long time to be elected by the people, not the big business and industry giants, and he is trying to put reasonable controls on them, requiring them to deal with some of the negative effects they are having on our nation and its people, especially children and their ability to learn.

One of the elements that allowed slavery to flourish was the premise that black people were less than human and not intelligent enough to take care of themselves and this lessens the guilt that should have come with this practice. President Obama's obvious intelligence and ability to identify problems and propose solutions proves all of this wrong and transfers guilt back on to the guilty. He also is trying to put reasonable controls on capitalism.

An example of this is in the most recent catastrophic capitalistic failure, when the entire system was disintegrating. While I agree that single capitalistic institutions should be allowed to fail, it would have been unconscionable for President Obama to allow Wall Street, the insurance industry, the banking industry, the auto industry, and the real estate industry all to fail at the same time. If this would have happened, he would have been blamed for the greatest depression the world has ever seen, even though the entire mess had taken more than sixty years of destroying regulations designed to keep this from happening.

At this time, we see big business holding back on employing people, making the economy worse, just to see the election of those politicians who will keep laws controlling pollution and wages from being passed. Pollution and insufficient wages have an effect on children and learning.

President Clinton

President Clinton tried to put controls on so much of capitalism that it would take many pages to name them all, so it is obvious why he was targeted for impeachment and destruction!

The people above are able to identify serious national problems and come up with solutions, but the solutions don't often make capitalists happy!

Chapter 26
Evaluating Teachers and Merit Pay

The administrator as the evaluator

Too often, the administrator-evaluators in education are those who left the classroom because they knew that they were never going to be good teachers, so they went into administration.

Many times, these people do not know what a good teacher is, but they go on to evaluate teachers and perhaps even advise presidents, as may have been the case in the Bush administration with the No Child Left Behind Act, where the foundation is that all children are equal. Anyone who has ever taught knows that that is not true, yet a national program was built on this untruth.

In the Obama administration, someone has advised him that merit pay is the answer to improving public education. Whoever it was must never have worked in public education, or that party would know the difficulties in evaluating teachers because of the enormous number of variables involved. There is the possibility, because of the politics involved, that the person being rated high may be one of the worst teachers, and the others teachers in the school know this, making morale plunge and finally destroying public education.

The politics of evaluating teachers

Too often, favorites are played with teachers. A good-looking young female teacher working under a horny male administrator could be given classes with no learning problems or discipline problems. Maybe an administrator doesn't put learning or discipline problems in the classroom of his golf partner. These are just examples of why tenure is necessary, and why there needs to be documentation before dismissal.

Evaluating teachers

Terms like evaluating and testing indicate a degree of scientific control, where there are givens and equals, and where the results would be the variable. An example would be if we were to evaluate two building contractors. We would give each of them the exact same blueprint for a building. The blueprint would have all the information to build the building, such as the plan of the building, all the building materials, grades, nailing schedule, cabinets, plumbing, electrical, roofing, and so forth. The only variable would be the workmanship of the contractors being evaluated.

When we try to evaluate a teacher, we have nothing *but* variables affecting the teacher's evaluation. There are twenty to forty or more different students within the class and there are variables with in the physical setting the teachers are given to teach in. Student performance can change from moment to moment or day to day, depending on home problems, diet, sleep, and so on. The materials, texts, libraries, computers, and rooms the teachers are given are typically quite different. There may be a noisy freeway outside one teacher's room and not another's. The out-of-class assignments of teachers vary as well; some may be assigned to be in charge of the school annual, newspaper, after-school sports, chaperoning dances, and lunch duty; and some teachers, like English teachers, may have as much as one hundred hours of grading papers a week.

When I was teaching junior high in what was considered about the roughest school in the city, eighteen new teachers walked out the first week of school, and I had two classes of thirty-four students each. As mentioned previously, they were labeled "special and adjustments," and that meant that every child in each of those classes had a serious learning or discipline problem, or both. The best teacher in the world would not have been evaluated as a good teacher in these circumstances, but it did help the students and me when I got a full-time aide.

I have seen some average teachers refuse to take students with low IQs or discipline problems, and these students are given to other teachers, who consequently will not look like the best teachers. I know of several instances where the teachers taking the difficult students were black, and the very teachers who got rid of the difficult students were then critical of the teachers who took on the problems.

Evaluating teachers is almost impossible when there are so many variables and no givens or equal values in the evaluation. The only way that I can think of to be fair to the teacher is for the person doing the firing to take over the exact and complete teacher assignment and if the person doing the evaluation can show significant improvement with all the same "givens," then dismissal may be in order.

Merit pay and teacher morale

Teachers are very much aware of the politics between teachers—and between teachers and administrators—and of all the many variables involved with trying to evaluate teachers. I believe President Obama has had bad advice in this area, perhaps by someone who has never worked in public education.

It is my opinion that nothing can destroy morale in a school more than merit pay, as the teachers in a school know well who has unusually difficult assignments that may never make that teacher look good, and the others who may look good truly are not. In the end, it could also destroy the public school systems. Because of all the variables and political implications of evaluating teachers, I would hope that officials would become informed on the ramifications of these programs and the possible negative effects involved.

I would also be suspect of higher-up officials who advise politicians to promote programs that are based on all children being equal. It just is not so, and that is why I would question whoever advised President Bush on his No Child Left Behind program.

Lastly, when a school seems to be doing well, check to see if they are choosing only students with motivated parents and students; see if they eliminate students with learning and discipline problems, as religious and charter schools sometimes do. There must be motivated teachers, administrators, parents, and students to overcome the many learning problems faced by our nation. The problems did not just happen; they have taken many years to develop and cannot be solved fast or easily.

Burn out

Teaching is so intense that often the best teachers burn out over time! I feel that instead of spending money on merit pay, it would be better to provide full-time aides in every classroom, essentially having two adults in every classroom. One way to do this without spending money is to require all people in teacher education in colleges to spend one year *full time*, not just an hour a day, in the classroom of a master teacher. The student teacher might just have one evening class at the college a week to coordinate things, but would be full time in a classroom for one school year. This would not only give the student teacher a better experience, but it would go a long way in helping to prevent teacher burnout for the master teacher. Putting the money into teacher aides instead of merit pay would also avoid destroying teacher morale, and I believe it would encourage teachers who may be slacking off to get their acts together and do a better job, for they would have someone else in the classroom, watching them and giving them moral support as well as helping with all the work. The aide could also take care of discipline problems without the teacher having to stop teaching to do so. They also might do some remedial work either during class time or after school. The list of possibilities could be greatly expanded.

Another way to provide two adults in every classroom would be to have all citizens give two years to the country. I describe this more in the next chapter.

Tenure

Teaching is so intense while in the classroom, and all teachers must know before they go to bed each night what maybe two hundred students will be doing each minute of the next day. A teacher will teach for an average of three years before receiving tenure. During this time, teachers can be dismissed without documentation, and many teachers realize that they were not cut out to be teachers, so they quit on their own. After receiving tenure, there must be documentation as to why the teacher is being dismissed, and this seems reasonable in light of all the variables and politics mentioned above. It usually is not hard to document when a teacher is actually bad, as long as there is a good administrator doing it.

Firing teachers

While some teachers should be fired, no teachers should be fired by anyone who could not do a better job than they are doing. As I mentioned earlier, the person doing the firing should be required to take over the teacher's class for at least, say, two months, without transferring out any of the students with problems, and then he or she should use the same standards on himself or herself that were used to evaluate the teacher.

Too often, teachers who look good transfer out the problem students, and that just means that some other teacher has an overload of problem students, or sometimes the student just drops out. Again, teachers are often evaluated by administrators who couldn't make it in the classroom, so they went into administration and don't have a clue about how to improve learning in the classroom.

One of the worst things happening in education now is thinking that schools can be run like businesses, where the materials business are given to work with are of equal quality. Children are not all equal, and every teacher is going to have a different set of materials to work with, yet teachers are expected to have an identical product. Having a businessperson evaluate teachers is ridiculous, as I cannot think of another industry where the workers have no control over the materials they are given to produce a product.

Chapter 27

Solutions

Capitalists think of people as machines that are all alike, and this is just not true. Each person has a different intelligence, different interests, different psychological makeup, and different physical characteristics. All these conditions must be taken into consideration during the learning process.

I truly believe that all along the learning path, students should be evaluated for their potential to gain from further academic exposure, and if they can't gain, maybe they should be put into a vocational or working situation that would let them perform and not fail, as they are doing in school. The student is probably failing for good reason, and another failure is not going to fix the problem.

Students with very low IQs can succeed by working in the food court at a local shopping center, clearing and cleaning tables, picking up trash, and so forth. Why waste money and time trying to get children to perform academically when there simply is not the potential to learn? Some students are not able to assimilate, process, and apply knowledge, so we should stop trying to make the impossible happen.

All administrators or critics of education should be required to spend one year, full time, in a difficult classroom situation before trying to solve learning problems.

Children should be given tests to determine aptitude and interests, which will determine the areas they are likely to do best in, and then teachers can teach to these groups. At James Boys Ranch, students were organized into reading levels in each subject so that they could actually start performing immediately. The students who could not function in their regular classes were removed, and those were the ones I was given to deal with. Classroom teachers cannot be expected to try to teach children with learning disabilities who usually end up causing discipline problems. We are starting to do this nowadays with what are called magnet schools, which teach to a person's interests. Why try to teach every child higher math when only those going into math and science careers would ever use this information?

Get rid of "No Child Left Behind"

"Horse manure" is a descriptive term often used by President Truman, and one day someone asked his wife, Bess, why she couldn't get him to use another term besides manure. She looked at her and said, "It has taken me forty years to get him to say manure!"

The reason most teachers and I would use the term manure to describe the No Child Left Behind act is because its very premise is that all people are created equal, and this is just not true. No Child Left Behind assumes that all children will come to a teacher with exactly the same knowledge and capacity for learning, all equal and regulated by tests, and they are expected to leave equal, and the test results should show this. This means that a teacher teaches to the lowest level in an attempt to bring them up to meet the test requirements. The teacher may be teaching students who have emotional problems that affect learning or low IQs so they don't have the capacity to learn. The most descriptive term for this program is *manure*!

When I was nearing the end of my teaching career, I was assigned to teach two art classes. The first one was one of the best I had ever had, but the next hour had more than its share of discipline problems. In an art class, students need to get out of their seats, so problems are amplified. A student teacher was assigned to the first class, and she was a middle-aged divorcée who had to begin supporting herself.

I told her that she would be teaching the class, but I would always be there because for a teacher a really good class is very rewarding. She then told me that she would stay for the second hour and help all she could with that class. This second adult in the classroom is preferable in all classrooms—but necessary when dealing with children with discipline problems.

When a teacher has a good class, it is exciting, and it makes teaching worthwhile and rewarding. She was an excellent student teacher, but she said that she would not have learned anything if she had not watched me deal with the difficult students. If she had the difficult class, she might have failed her student teaching assignment or dropped out of the teacher prep program.

This is the reason merit pay is not feasible. The students each teacher is dealing with can vary, and even the best teachers might look bad when dealing with students with learning and emotional problems. It can also work the other way; an average teacher with a class of high IQs and no learning problems or discipline problems can look better than he or she actually is!

Here in the San Diego area, two beautiful girls were raped and murdered recently by John Gardener III. During his trial, he started to tell about the abuse he had suffered in his life, and the media immediately accused him of trying to excuse himself for his criminal behavior. While he should not be excused, we should listen.

I think we would find that the same things that are causing learning problems in our students are what are causing so much criminal behavior. The bad students frequently turn into criminals that cause so much heartache and we need to start identifying these causes and trying to change them to protect future generations from what is happening now.

A new two year draft program including both men and women could solve many national problems

Two areas that make good places for people to serve are the military and the Peace Corps. The other two that I propose developing would be in education and the medical fields. All four of these areas have an enormous number of opportunities as far as exploratory work and training are concerned. All four of these areas would provide a healthy, cheap workforce in areas that could desperately use low-cost help so needed services can be delivered to all our citizens, and the workers would be gaining experience and knowledge in areas that they might make their life's work.

A national service program would also act as an exploratory work experience program

Let's look at each one of these areas individually and discuss how they could be used to serve not only the nation but the participants as well. All the people in our country would have to give two years to the nation, and they could choose between the four areas either before or after college. In some instances, their assistance might help pay for their college education—for instance, in the medical fields, where the costs are so extreme.

The military has been and could be even a better place for exploratory work experience, which they have been doing successfully for years. The military offers excellent educational programs that can also be used in civilian life, but hopefully more people would decide to stay in the military and lessen the need for civilian military contractors. It seems to me as though civilian contractors tend to be war profiteering with their pay so much more than people in the military.

The Peace Corps is already organized, and from what I have seen, it provides great training and some exploratory work experience. This is usually a wonderful experience, and I have seen many participants want to make this their life's work. This is also a good investment for our country in creating good relations between countries, which is a better way of helping another country, than just giving money to a government that might help the leader stay in power when the people of the county would get rid of that leader if they were not being supported by an outside entity.

The Education Corps, for people who chose it, would mean hands-on exploratory work experience, providing that second adult in the classroom. Hopefully, some of these people would decide to go into teaching, but they would at least be providing moral support for some burned-out former good teachers, helping them return to good teaching. They could also help with discipline problems, grade papers, tutor, help contact parents when necessary, and generally assist in a host of other areas. This would also likely help a marginally good teacher become much better. I cannot enumerate and exaggerate the good that could come from such a program.

The Medical Corps is one of the other areas that would provide a good variety of help in an area that could use low-cost assistance to professionals, and at the same time, the participants would be gaining good training and experience. I believe that this program would be especially effective if every public college incorporated a teaching hospital and every two-year community college had a clinic associated with it. These hospitals and clinics would not only train doctors and nurses, but would give work experience to these people. This would also give low-income persons and people on Medicare a place that would cost the country less for their medical care.

The above would provide a wide variety of jobs that people could do for their two-year obligation to national service.

Data bank of people with psychological disorders

Everyone who enters the national service program would be screened, just as we screen for the military and the Peace Corps now, so we could be developing a data bank of people with emotional problems. While this means giving up some freedoms, I believe that because everyone would be required to participate, it should be acceptable. I also believe that when a person has a problem that makes him ineligible to serve, this is the time to require that he or she get help with problems such as drug addiction, clinical depression, ADD, ADHD, dyslexia, and the host of other problems that are becoming more and more treatable.

We know that our prisons have an inordinate number of inmates with all kinds of psychological and learning disorders, and they are not being helped in prison. In fact, they are probably getting worse. Then there are those with much more serious psychological and mental disorders. All these people need to be diagnosed earlier and receive treatment, because in many ways, they are taking our nation down. These people could spend at least a part of their two-year obligation getting treatment. As it is now, we wait until they have committed a crime and then put them in jail, where they get no help with their problem. Moreover, prison is one of the most expensive programs we have, and it will probably bankrupt the country eventually.

Many fine professionals, such as Dr. Drew Pinsky, could come together and develop an excellent program to help many people and stop much of the negative behavior that we are now putting up with in this country. Teachers know when they have students with serious problems, but it is not easy for them to get involved with reporting these problems. *We must come up with bold programs and start implementing them; our problems didn't just happen overnight, and they are not going to solve themselves.*

Positive gangs

The national service program, with each of its four areas, would actually provide positive gangs, which the military already is, for all of our young citizens. This program would allow all citizens to develop a feeling of ownership and belonging that is so necessary in everyones' lives.

Educators had it right many years ago when they provided something for everyone to come to school for. They provided a wide range of subjects, activities, clubs, and after-school activities, which I like to think of as positive gangs. In the communities, there were other positive gangs run by the Boy Scouts, Girl Scouts, YMCAs, churches, and the list could go on and on. These gangs provided many positive things in the community, for there was at least one place in society where each child could find success and a sense of belonging. In recent years, we have lost this sense of belonging to anything, not even to a family, and I believe this is why so many turn to negative gangs, drugs, and crime.

The attitude now is to fail them, and many failures in their lives could be why they are not learning. Failing children does not motivate them to do better, and it does not address the reason why they are not achieving.

If they simply cannot succeed, then it would be much more productive to find a place for them where they can succeed and be productive. The variety of subjects and activities in our public schools has been curtailed lately in the name of the economy, but the effect on society has been much more expensive.

Dropping out and joining a gang should not be an option, and children who cannot perform should be placed in programs where they can at least be productive citizens. I know this is taking their freedom away in a sense, but this would be better than having them in destructive gangs or in prison. Forming positive gangs with positive outcomes, in the form of a national service program, could make our nation the envy of the world.

When I was young, our church had several positive gangs that I belonged to. There was a group of us who ushered every Sunday, which I did for five years, and that made us all feel like we were a more important part of this organization. I also went in during the week and set up the church marquee that announced what the sermon would be for the next Sunday. In addition, I was also active in the church youth group that met on Sunday evenings, where each person took a turn developing a short religious program, and then we frequently went to different homes afterward for social get-togethers and refreshments. We also had retreats at the church camp, as well as dances and beach parties. This positive gang still gets together, even after more than fifty years—unfortunately, sometimes for memorial services.

This church also had a program where several groups of high school students, with adult counselors, traveled from Southern California during the Easter week to work on Native American churches in Arizona. We learned the importance of organizing to prepare food to feed the group and procure the supplies and have the organizational skills to complete a job. The Indian children frequently worked with us, and it gave us a wonderful opportunity to get to know people that we would probably never meet if it weren't for this activity. The young people on these work teams came away not only with new close friends from home but also knowledge of people that have been misrepresented in our society for too long. They came away with loving, caring relationships with people that they had considered "different," and perhaps inferior.

Activities of this nature give their participants an important sense of belonging. If a child is not succeeding academically, some other productive activity should be found for him so he doesn't leave school and join or form negative gangs.

When I worked in the Work Experience Program in the high school where I taught, we developed a program called the Exploratory Work Experience Program, where students could go to observe and work, nonpaid, in a large number of professions. These areas were things like fire departments, navy communications, plumbers, electricians, office helpers, veterinary hospitals, telephone companies, TV stations, and many other places where students could experience work in the real world and begin to feel a part of it.

This was a time of success for those not finding academic success at school. This program also offered them the opportunity to explore a subject before spending a lot of money training for something they might not truly care for.

In this way, employers could get to know their potential future employees, and many students were hired because they had worked in the program. This is why I would include an exploratory work program as part of a national service program.

Why do we insist on keeping children in failing situations when they have probably had a lifetime of failing? Let them find something else where they can be productive citizens and not turn to negative gangs.

The Exploratory Work Experience Program is just one way that local businesses and industry can aid in the learning process. Another example is when we had a principal who developed an educational foundation of interested parents, students, local citizenry, and people from business and industry, and the goal was to support education at that school in any way we could think of. We had fundraisers to raise money for special new equipment in classrooms, and an architectural firm was developing plans to remodel one of the older buildings into a little theater, something the school had never had. They were even going to provide at least some of the funds! I have never seen a more dedicated, active group of people, and it was exciting for me just to be a part of it.

Class size

Unless class size is examined, those who are not teachers cannot have any concept of the effect this can have on the learning process. The following is an example: If an English teacher has forty students in each of his five classes, this amounts to two hundred students per day. The teacher has to prepare to teach and then teach for the five hours, and so far, this doesn't sound too bad, but there is a problem. All two hundred students will have at least one assignment per week, and it would not be unreasonable for an English teacher to assign a writing assignment that would take a half hour to grade for each student. This would mean that the one assignment would take the teacher one hundred hours to grade in a single week! This may sound extreme, but with the cuts almost everywhere in our country, this is getting to be the norm.

While it takes time to grade papers, there are many other tasks teachers have to do as well, such as meeting with parents and others, chaperoning athletic events and dances, and so on.

Parent involvement

Parents should be involved in their children's education, but sometimes, for various reasons, this is not possible, and sometimes the parent is the problem, as many teachers experience on a daily basis. The parent just has too many problems of their own or just not enough time to be a positive influence in the learning process.

Twenty-four-hour schools

Sometimes it is better if children are just away from home and all the distractions that family and community life present. Again, James Boys Ranch is a good example of controlled living changing children's lives and how they function, not only in a learning situation but in providing for their own survival as well. There are twenty-four hour schools being developed where the students live in, and their learning is the major thing in their lives.

The SEED program in Washington, D.C., is an example of an excellent twenty-four-hour live-in program for turning around learning problems, and it has many similarities to the James Boys Ranch that I worked with during the 1960s. Because it has taken hundreds of years to create the problems we have in education, if we are really serious about improving learning, it will take even more extreme measures than this, but this is an excellent beginning. Children and their families in the SEED program are at least functional enough to realize that education is important; too many families are too dysfunctional to give any importance to education. Perhaps the problems many families face nowadays force them to place the priority of education lower on their lists of importance.

There is a need for more medical facilities to treat learning problems, both physical and psychological
Again, I think we may need to think in terms of attaching a medical training and research facility to almost every university and community college to help solve these learning problems. Research in our universities usually develops cures for health problems; drug companies only develop drugs that control the symptoms, and they need to be purchased for life!

It is my opinion that Medicare should not pay for anything like organ transplants. If a person wants to have such a thing at an advanced age, he should purchase insurance for this purpose. There should be no heroic end-of-life procedures done at Medicare's expense. We must begin to look at death as part of the living experience! Too often, we are putting our loved ones and eventually ourselves through unnecessary trauma and pain.

We need to break the neurotic chain that is the cause of so many of our problems, but that won't be easy—that same neurosis is what feeds capitalism!

Summary

I have mentioned in this book what I believe to be capitalistic needs that over centuries are the causes of the learning problems in our country. These needs must have reasonable regulations placed on them or our nation will suffer severely. I have repeated these needs below and included some of the controls that are needed so that we don't keep making the problems worse.

1. A large quantity *of cheap raw materials.*
Regulations: Control waste of these materials; keep them out of food chain, air, water, and so forth.

2. A large quantity of *cheap energy.*
Regulations: Conserve energy in every way possible, and an example is the need to primarily transport people and products via rail rather than roadways. Siemens advertises that their 220-miles-per-hour passenger trains get the equivalent of 700 miles to the gallon per passenger. CSX says one freight train can pull 280 trucks off our congested highways. Trains are three times more energy efficient than trucks and carry a ton of freight 436 miles on a gallon of fuel. Moreover, they can run on other things besides oil.

3. A large quantity of *cheap labor.* Slavery is no longer acceptable, and if wages are too low for too many people, there is no one to buy the products that capitalism produces. This is what brought about slavery, and it has now been replaced by labor from Mexico, China, and India. We must find ways to pay people a living wage.

4. A large number of *neurotic, compulsive consumers* capable of purchasing the goods produced by capitalism. There is a vicious circle here because capitalism has been responsible for the creation of most neurotics and all the accompanying problems, so they are creating their own clientele.
Regulations: Capitalism will never take responsibility for the problems it has created, so government programs to reverse damages that have taken place over many hundreds of years will have to be designed and implemented.

It will take some drastic programs to end the neurotic chain and an example of something that might help would be to divide our cities into small villages with all social services, fire, police, religious, educational organizations with representatives from each area meeting regularly to help people deal with problems early. If there is a learning problem, get help. If there is a dropout from school, get him appropriate work and into a positive gang. Hopefully, the problem can be identified and solved before it gets to the dropout stage.

It is as if a big circle of neurotics had a need for a love substitute, and sugar was one, so they created slavery to produce sugar, producing more neurotics in the process!

Sugar is so refined that shouldn't it be controlled as we do drugs? If we ever want to get our health-care costs under control, we may have to do just that. This would put big business in a tizzy, as the addition of sugar to so much of what we consume brings in large amounts of money for these businesses.

This is just a quick idea, but we must have some serious think tanks of people with experience dealing with children's problems that could come up with some solutions. We can no longer say that this is "their" problem, because these problems can take down a nation. It is in our national interest for *all* of our citizens to have access to good, healthy food, health care, education, and so forth—while avoiding exposure to toxic chemicals and traumatic experiences.

5. Capitalism wants *no regulations*; they get in the way of profits. There is the need to pollute without being responsible for the cost of cleanup. Disposing of trash and the cleanup of by-products and chemicals that pollute the land, rivers, lakes, oceans, and air are things that capitalists want socialized, and when they are done using people, they are left as human rubble.
Regulations: The days of the pundits protecting capitalists from regulation *must end*! Businesses and industries must be taxed for *pollution, disposal, and recycling of what their businesses create.* There are islands of plastic in our oceans, streams and lakes filled with toxins, and our cities are filled with polluted air. The government and the people should not be responsible for these messes.

6. With capitalism, there is no overall *national plan;* anything that can make money goes, with no regard for what is best for people or the

long term of the nation. The tearing up of our electric rail transportation systems and putting this traffic on highways is a good example of this. The rest of the world has high-speed economical public transportation, but in the United States, the auto industry and the neurotic needs of our people still control transportation. We are left with polluting, wasteful transportation systems that have turned our cities into parking structures and our highways into parking lots, while filling our air, water, and land with pollutants. There is more scientific evidence all the time that these pollutants are part of the reason children don't learn.

Long-term national plans must be put in place to ensure that we have systems that are the least polluting, the most economical, use the least energy, and are the least destructive to our valuable land as possible. We did commit the greatest genocide in the history of the world to get this land; the least we can do is take care of it.

7. Capitalists seldom take responsibility for the pollution they create, chemical, environmental, and human rubble. Saying that the minimum wage should be lower and the rich should pay lower taxes are the talking points of capitalists.

Regulations: We should take pride in our nation and make sure all our citizens have proper wages, health care, and education, to name a few of our people's needs.

Many of us think that when we stop doing the things that cause learning problems, that will solve the problems, but once a problem has been created, it not only affects that person but many generations to come. The problems just keep getting passed along either sociologically, psychologically, or through altered DNA.

In order to examine what was done wrong and what is causing our problems today, we must look at the past. The interesting thing is that when we do so, we are criticized for being anti-American! This, of course, just confirms the fact that our past was bad—and it is not hard to find answers to the *why* and the *who* of the problem. The big problem now is how we undo what has taken centuries to create.

In critiquing the problem, I came up with what could be some of the causes affecting learning, and this begins with recognizing that not all children are equal. I have also tried to describe some of the neurological problems that affect learning, showing how the proliferation of chemicals into our daily lives can have a negative effect on learning. Then I presented some of the historic sociological and present sociological lifestyles that could also damage the learning process.

Even if some teachers had just a few students with minor problems in the different areas that I have presented, they would have a difficult time meeting the requirements being placed upon them at this time. The other students in a classroom could be excelling if the teacher did not have to spend so much time dealing with the learning difficulties that they are not trained, nor should they be trained, to deal with. Teachers need all the time they can get just being good teachers to good students. Other professionals should be taking care of the psychological, sociological, and learning disabilities affecting the learning of children with problems.

The whole world needs to control harmful chemicals and detrimental substances. The whole world needs to start dealing with the serious social problems that are causing so much strife and affecting learning.

It is sometimes assumed that teachers can just inject knowledge with a syringe as a doctor would a vaccination, but knowledge is only learned when the learner is willing and ready, and has the aptitude and interest.

You can lead a horse to water, but you can't make him drink. Likewise, you can introduce children to knowledge, but you can't make them learn.

Administrators may claim to be improving learning in nonperforming schools, but too often they are just manipulating the statistics or not including students with learning problems. Sometimes even charter schools transfer out students with problems, so it is hard to evaluate teachers, schools, and administrators.

Public education is just the canary trying to warn a nation that history is catching up with it, and that there are some serious problems that need to be addressed. They will not be until we start looking at the real problem, which is capitalism's needs, and the effect these needs have on children and learning!

The solutions are more complicated than getting rid of bad teachers, instituting merit pay, designing new curriculum, or building new schools, but the important thing is undoing hundreds of years of destructive forces upon our children, which have had and are still having such negative effects on learning.

Hopefully, I have helped the reader understand some of the complexities in why public education seems not to be doing a good job. I also hope that I have given some ideas on how to solve some of the problems. Most of my ideas come from my experiences, not from scientific fact, but science seems to be strengthening my ideas every day.

Epilogue

Uncle Bob and Aunt Monica are at the river for the winter, and it's just before Christmas. The ravages of multiple sclerosis and strokes have taken their toll on Aunt Monica, and she is no longer able to talk. She only has the use of her left arm, and she can only shuffle her feet enough to get around in her wheelchair. She always liked to send Christmas gifts to everyone in the family, and she had tried all night to communicate to Uncle Bob that he needed to make sure that they had not forgotten anyone.

They had been married for sixty-five years, and Uncle Bob was now eighty-five years old. He was still lifting Monica out of the wheelchair, onto the toilet, and into bed. He was bathing her as well.

The next morning after breakfast, Uncle Bob was going to make the trip up the long driveway and through the forest to get the mail. Aunt Monica motioned that she was going to sit on the deck for a while. That was where we always had our family pictures taken, and there was the beautiful view of the river curving through the valleys. Many times, we had watched the full moon rise up over the mountains on the far side of the river, and during the day, the hummingbirds would come and sip from their feeders. Chipmunks would steal seed from the other feeder.

Uncle Bob got the mail, and as he walked down the ruts of the driveway, with its glistening riverbed pebbles, and ferns and huckleberry brush alongside, he had to be wondering how much longer he would be able to be the caregiver he had been for so many years.

He entered the living room and through the windows saw Aunt Monica on the deck with her head down; a cerebral accident had snuffed out her view of the beautiful Rogue and would soon stop her breathing.

Driving the Oregon coast with its spectacular views, when you get to the south side of the beautiful arched bridge at Gold Beach, there is a road that goes inland, and if you drive up the river for about an hour, you will come to Agnes, Oregon. Just a short distance farther, you will make a sharp left turn onto a high bridge over the Rogue River. Turn right and take the road nearest the river, continuing until you get to Foster Bar. Go just a little farther and there will be Foster Creek and the clearing. The big Petinger house burned many years ago, and Aunt Monica's little one-room schoolhouse has been gone about as long. But if you are there on a spring day after a shower, you can still see, sparkling in the sun, the yearly return of *a square of daffodils*!

www.ingramcontent.com/pod-product-compliance
Lightning Source LLC
Chambersburg PA
CBHW022245290526
45785CB00015B/175